Preschool Art

PreSchool Art

"It's the process not the product."

By MaryAnn Kohl

Illustrations by K. Whelan Dery

gryphon house
Beltsville, MD

Dedication

Dedicated in memory of my grandmother, Mary Geanne Faubion Wilson, the first published author I ever knew, who sparked by imagination when she told me that angels made my freckles when they kissed me on the nose as I slept.

Acknowledgments

I would like to thank my editor, Kathy Charner, for her ability to organize my writing schedule for *Preschool Art* and also her humor and kindness in our editor-author relationship. Sometimes I think we were just having too much fun to call this work! In addition, I would like to thank the owners of Gryphon House, Leah and Larry Rood, for their support and friendship, and their belief in this book and in me. Most important, my thanks go to my husband, Michael, and my daughters, Hannah and Megan, who keep my mind clear, tell me when I've been wonderful or when I haven't and remind me of what is most important in life.

Copyright © 1994 MaryAnn Kohl
Published by Gryphon House, Inc.
10726 Tucker Street, Beltsville MD 20702

Cover Design: Bryan Linkous, Irv Kline and Associates
Cover Photography: Pam Soorenko, Photo Group

Library of Congress Cataloging in Publication Data

Kohl, Mary Ann F
  Preschool art : "It's the process, not the product." / by MaryAnn Kohl ; Illustrations by K. Whelan Dery.
      p.   cm.
  Includes indexes.
  ISBN 0-87659-168-3 : $19.95
      1. Art--Study and teaching (Preschool) -- Handbooks, manuals, etc.
  I. Dery, K. Whelan, ill. II. Title
  LB1140.5.A7K64   1994
  372.5'2--dc20

                                             94-15714
                                                 CIP

A Special Note About Process Art

Dear Fellow Artists,

Welcome to the world of process art, a world you already know quite well if you have ever scribbled with crayons on paper just to see the colors mix and swirl! Do you like smearing your hand through cool, smooth fingerpaint and watching colors mix on the paper? Do you enjoy finding interesting collage materials and gluing them on silver foil? Then you will love Preschool Art! It is filled with months of art experiences for every child, ages three through six (and older brother and sisters, mom, dads and grandparents, too) to explore.

"Process not product" means that you can explore art materials and enjoy what happens. You don't have to copy what an adult makes or even try to make something a friend has made. There is no right or wrong way for these art ideas to turn out; there is only YOUR way. YOU are the artist.

Have you ever spread cool, smooth fingerpaint across a cookie sheet? Well, you should try it..it feels wonderful and the most exciting things happen to the paint. I won't tell you what because I don't want to spoil the surprise of the process of art. When you try fingerpainting on a cookie sheet, don't concern yourself with what you should make. Just enjoy the doing. That's the whole idea of process art.

Have you ever melted crayons on a warming tray? This book tells you how to get started, and the process will amaze you! Some very strange and wonderful things happen to crayon when it is liquid. I know you'll enjoy the creative process of discovering just what happens!

Oh, I almost forgot to tell you something important! It's perfectly alright if you don't want to save whatever art experience you just finished. You can throw it away or take it home or cut it up into little pieces and glue them on something else! Simply enjoy creating.

I hope you have a wonderful time with the process of art as you discover, create and explore your way through a whole year full of art experiences. Oh, and don't forget to help clean up!

Process, not Product!

MaryAnn Kohl

Using the Icons

Each activity has up to five icons to make the projects in Preschool Art more useable and accessible for the artist, care-giver, teacher or parent. These icons are suggestions, subject to your personal and individual modifications or changes based on your experience and needs. Experiment with materials, vary suggested techniques or modify projects to suit the needs and abilities of each artist or each adult. Creative variation is part of the fun of providing preschool art experiences.

Age

Age indicates the general age range where a child can create and explore independently, that is, without much adult assistance. The "& UP" means that children this age and all ages older should be comfortable doing the project. However, children younger than the age suggestion can also do the project with adult assistance. Children do not always fit the standard developmental expectations of a particular age, so decide which projects suit individual children and their specific abilities and needs.

Planning/Preparation

Easy   Moderate   Involved

This icon indicates the degree of planning or preparation time an adult will need to collect materials, set up the activity or supervise the activity. Icons shown indicate planning and preparation time that is easy, moderate or involved.

Help

The help icon indicates the artist may need extra assistance from another child or from an adult during this activity.

Caution

This icon appears for all activities that suggest the use of sharp, hot or electrical materials. All activities require supervision, but activities with the caution icon need extra care. For steps an adult should perform, the word "adult" is in bold type.

Author's Favorite

MaryAnn Kohl's favorite projects are shown with a star. Favorites are selected on the basis of one of three criteria: 1) extra fun, 2) extra fascinating or 3) extra easy and creative.

Table of Contents

Table of Contents

Table of Contents

Table of Contents

9

Table of Contents

Introduction

It's the Process, not the Product

Young children "do" art for the experience, the exploration, the experimentation. In the "process" they discover mystery, creativity, joy, frustration. The resulting masterpiece, whether it be a sticky glob or meritorious gallery piece, is only a result to the young child, not the reason for doing art in the first place. Art allows children to explore and discover their world. Sometimes the process is merely feeling slippery paint on the fingers, other times it is the mystery of colors blending or the surprise of seeing a realistic picture evolve when blobs were randomly placed. Art can be a way to "get the wiggles out" or to smash a ball of clay instead another child.

Sometimes adults unknowingly communicate to a child that the result is the most important aspect of art. Encourage discovery and process by talking with a child about his or her artwork.

- *Tell me about your painting.*
- *What part did you like best?*
- *You've used many colors.*
- *Did you enjoy making this?*
- *How did the paint feel?*
- *The yellow looks so bright next to the purple!*
- *How did you make such a big design?*
- *I see the painting is brown. What colors did you use?*

Providing interesting materials and watching what a child can do on his or her own is better than saying, "Paint a green fish in blue water." It can be far more exciting to paint on a piece of frozen paper or to paint with a feather instead of a brush, with no idea of what will happen, than to follow an adult's idea of what to paint.

Process art is a wonder to behold. Watch the children discover their capabilities and the joy of creativity.

Using *Preschool Art*

Preschool Art is filled with over 200 process art experiences for young children. The first chapter in the book is called The Basics. These projects are basic art ideas every preschooler will want to experience. All the other projects in this book build on these basic art ideas. They can be done at any time during the year, experienced more than once (in fact many, many times) and they will always be of value to the developing young child.

The remaining four chapters are arranged by seasons and divided by months. For each month you will find approximately 20 art ideas using four art categories: drawing, painting, sculpting with dough and clay, and crafts/constructing. The first three categories are the most process oriented and open-ended art ideas. The constructing ideas are somewhat more craft than art, but still open-ended. Drawing indicates art ideas that involve pencils, crayons, pens and other drawing techniques such as drawing with glue, a finger in the sand or other unusual types of drawing. Painting could be painting with brushes or some other tool, using paint, food coloring or dye, or printing with a variety of materials. The sculpting projects involve using materials to make three dimensional art ideas using a wealth and variety of art materials commonly found in the home or classroom. The construction projects tend to lean

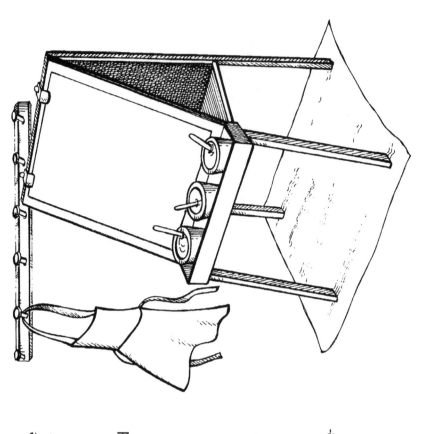

more towards crafts, but involve creative thinking in making puppets, wreaths, jewelry and other things.

There is one idea per page, complete with a materials list followed by steps in the art process with illustrations for each project. The upper page corner has icons that help the reader or artist quickly access the art idea with information on age, planning and preparation, safety and assistance needed. A side bar on the page tells the reader what type of art technique is featured in the project such as painting, sculpture or drawing. At the bottom of each page is the name of the month to which the project has been assigned.

By using the seasonal chapters it is possible to follow along through the book page by page, day by day and have plenty of process art experiences to last the entire year. However, it should be mentioned that choosing any project in the book at any time is also an exciting way to provide art for children.

Another way to select projects is by using the indexes. For instance, if you know you have tempera paint and glue, look up tempera paint or glue in the Materials Index. Find those projects that use those materials and begin to select one that suits you and the young artist. Another good use for the Materials Index is to help you select and save materials for your art center. Look through the index and note materials you have on hand as well as those you might start saving ahead of time.

Preschool Art is organized in a way to make process art experiences accessible, easy and developmentally appropriate. Provide the materials, stand back and enjoy the process of creative art!

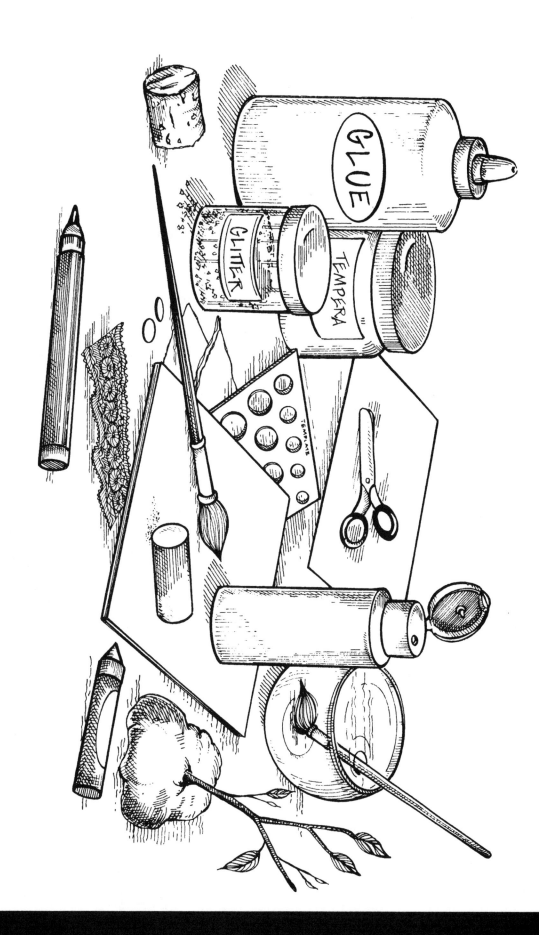

The Basics

Chalk Drawing

Materials

poster chalk or pastels (many colors)
paper
hair spray, optional

Art Process

1. Draw with colored chalk on paper.
2. When the drawing is complete, an **adult** can spray it outside with hair spray to "set" the chalk and help prevent smudging. However, the chalk will still smudge some.

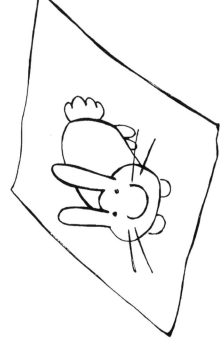

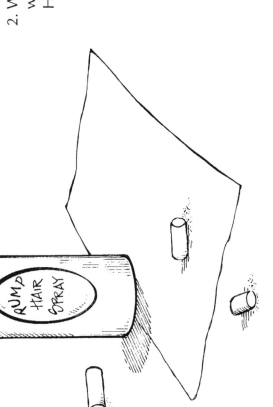

HINT · Chalk smudges, but chalk is beautiful. Allow experimentation with the unique qualities of chalk and don't be too concerned with its inherent messiness. Children need to learn the qualities of chalk, and smudging is one of them.

D R A W I N G

BASICS

Wet Chalk Drawing

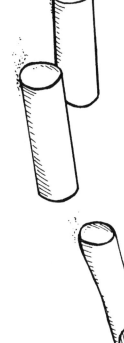

Materials

sugar solution (1/3 cup – 70g –sugar to 1 cup – 230ml – water)
container for sugar-water
poster chalk
paper
hair spray, optional

Art Process

1. Soak poster chalk overnight in sugar solution.
2. Draw with the wet chalk on paper.
3. The sugar-water helps brighten the chalk colors and keeps the drawing from smearing as much.
4. Dry the completed art project.
5. An **adult** can spray the completed drawing with hair spray (outside) if a non-smear drawing is desired.

Variation

- Dip the end of dry chalk into the sugar solution and draw with the dampened chalk.

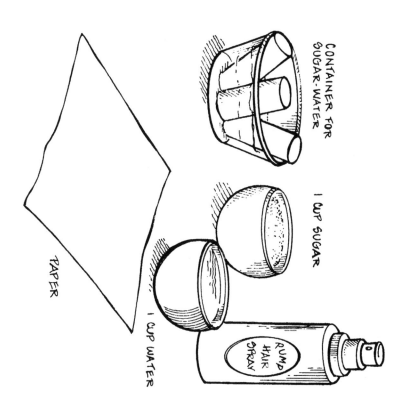

CONTAINER FOR SUGAR-WATER

1 CUP SUGAR

1 CUP WATER

PUMP HAIR SPRAY

PAPER

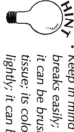

HINT • Keep in mind that chalk has unique qualities. It breaks easily; it smudges; it does not act like crayon; it can be brushed with a cotton ball, cotton swab or tissue; its colors can be blended, used brightly or lightly; it can be crushed and used as powder; powdered chalks can be mixed to make new chalk colors; it is messy and beautiful.

author's favorite

ALL ages

D R A W I N G

Dry Chalk Wet Paper

D R A W I N G

Materials

dish pan with about 4" (10 cm) of water in it
poster chalk or pastels
assorted papers
newspaper

Art Process

1. Dip the paper into the water, thoroughly coating it with water. Place it on a dry table.
2. Draw with dry chalk on the wet paper.
3. Experiment with different textures and types of paper.
4. Lift the completed project from the table.
5. Dry on newspaper for one or two days.

Variations

- Experiment with a paintbrush dipped in clear water on dry paper. Paint a design with the water and then draw with chalk on the watery design.
- Try rubbing the chalk drawing with a cotton ball or tissue to smudge, blend or smear.

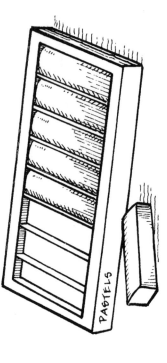

PASTELS

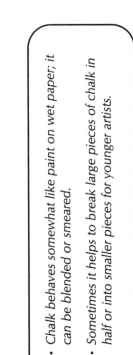

HINT
- Chalk behaves somewhat like paint on wet paper; it can be blended or smeared.
- Sometimes it helps to break large pieces of chalk in half or into smaller pieces for younger artists.

Chalk and Liquid Starch

Materials
small containers filled with liquid starch
small paintbrushes
poster chalk or pastels

Art Process
1. Brush the starch over the paper.
2. Draw on the paper with chalk.
3. The liquid starch brightens the chalk colors and reduces the powdery smudging of the chalk drawing. Drawing will still smudge.
4. Dry the completed art project.

Variation
- Dip the end of the chalk into the starch in the small container and draw on paper with dampened chalk.

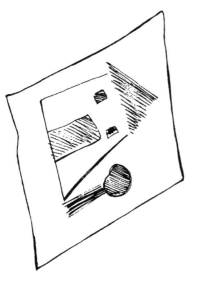

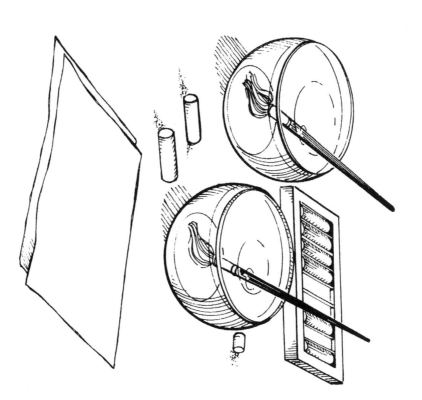

HINT
- Sometimes it helps to break big pieces of chalk in half or into smaller pieces for younger artists.
- Liquid starch can be saved and re-used for other projects requiring liquid starch.

Scribbler

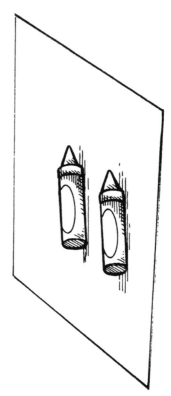

Materials
crayons
variety of papers

Art Process
1. Use big circular motions or free movement to create the outline of the artwork.
2. Color in the "holes" of the design, if desired.

Variations
- Use big paper for really big arm movements.
- Color to the rhythm of music.

HINT
- Expect lots of noise and very energetic arms because this project is really fun for young artists.
- Big arms movements also mean torn paper if a crayon catches the edge of the paper. Tape the paper to the table or easel.

BASICS

Free Drawing

Materials

crayons

variety of papers with different textures, colors and sizes

tables, easels or floor

Art Process

1. Use the crayon to draw on the paper.
2. Experiment with different textures, colors and sizes of papers.
3. Draw on paper placed on the flat surface of a table or floor, or use the upright surface of an easel.

Variations

· If the artist expresses some description about the drawing, the words can be written on the front or back of the drawing. You may want to write on a strip of paper that the artist can attach to the drawing themselves. Most art professionals feel it is best not to write directly on the artwork unless the artist specifically wishes it to be placed there.

· Provide other drawing tools such as charcoal, pencils, colored pencils, fine or wide point felt pens, pastels, chalk, fabric pens or any drawing tools available.

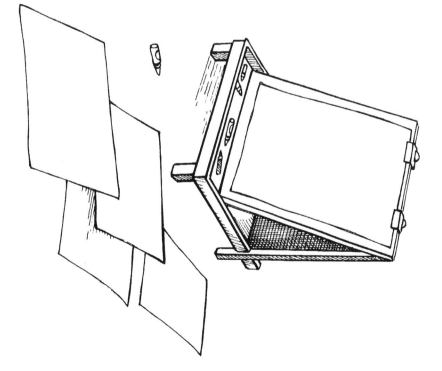

HINT

· Use Free Drawing often with young artists.
· The possibilities of Free Drawing are endless and varied

Crayon Rubbing

Materials

large, peeled crayons
butcher paper or construction paper
objects with textures for rubbings–pieces of yarn, pieces of
  sandpaper, shapes cut or torn from heavy paper, leaves,
  scraps of fabric glued to cards, other flat or textured items

Art Process

1. Place chosen objects under the heavy paper.
2. Tape the corners of the paper to the work surface to prevent
   shifting paper.
3. Holding the paper down with one hand, gently rub the flat side
   of the crayon over the covered objects.
4. An imprint of the covered object will appear on the paper.

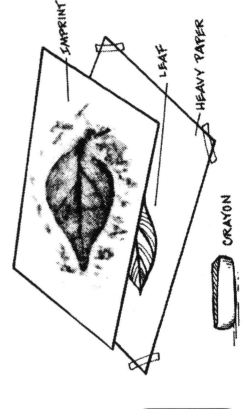

IMPRINT
LEAF
HEAVY PAPER
CRAYON

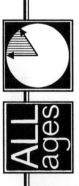

PAPER AND CRAYON

YARN

LEAVES

SANDPAPER

FABRIC SCRAP

PAPER SHAPE

HINT · Younger children will achieve varying degrees of
quality with rubbings. Age and experience will affect
the final outcome. Expect vigorous arm movements
and torn or wiggling paper if the project is not taped
to the work surface.

More Rub-a-Rub

Materials

large paper
large, peeled crayons
surfaces such as wood grain, tree bark, concrete, walls, bricks,
    tiles, leather and signs with raised or recessed letters
textures such as bumpy greeting cards, coins, license plates,
    corrugated cardboard, lace doilies, a comb, a piece of
    screen or a grill

Art Process

1. Place a large sheet of paper over any of the surfaces or textures
   listed above.
2. Rub the covered area with a large, peeled crayon held on its
   side.
3. Move on to another texture or surface, collecting the designs
   from as many as desired.

Variation

· Use the textures or rubbed designs to "color in" a picture. For
  example, rub over buttons for eyes, flocked wallpaper for
  clothing, tree bark for hair and so on.

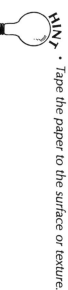

BRICK

10¢ COIN

COMB

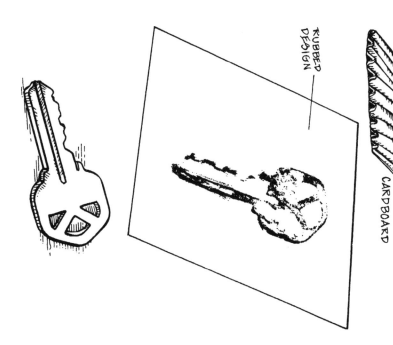

CARDBOARD

RUBBED DESIGN

HINT · Tape the paper to the surface or texture.

Body Trace

Materials

large sheets of butcher paper
crayon or felt pen
paints and brushes, optional
fabric scraps and glue, optional
large floor space
scissors

Art Process

1. The artist must lie down on a large sheet of butcher paper stretched out on the floor. Arms and legs should be spread out a little so they can be easily traced.
2. A second person takes a pen or crayon and traces the entire body of the artist including fingers, hair and other details.
3. When the tracing is complete, the artist can jump up and decide how to enhance the shape with paints, crayons, felt pens or fabric scraps and glue.
4. The object is to add all the features of the real person who was traced.
5. When the decorating and designing is complete, cut out the shape and tape it to the wall with feet touching the ground and the head at child height.

Variations

- A silhouette can be made using the same method. Use black paper and white chalk to complete this variation of the project.
- The shape can be decorated to look different from the person that was traced such as a being from outer space, a mother, a baker or some other character.

HINT
- Sometimes young artists are surprised and even disappointed with the tracing done by another person. You may wish to have teenagers, parents or other grown-up volunteers do the tracing rather than other young artists.

Mark Making

Materials

paper or other material to mark on

tools to make marks—pencils, chalk, crayons, markers or pastels

design tools such as a ruler, protractor, stencils, templates, lids, tops or objects to trace

Art Process

1. Select a drawing tool and start making marks on a selected material such as paper.
2. Explore and experiment with different marking and design tools. For instance, trace the lids of jars and overlap the circle shapes or make ruler lines of measured lengths with chalk. The possibilities are unlimited. The idea is to provide the markers and design tools and let the artists explore their imaginations.

Variation

• Make marks with paint. Dip the design tools in the paint and then place them on the paper to make a design. Make marks in the sand or dirt. Make footprints or hand prints. The possibilities are endless.

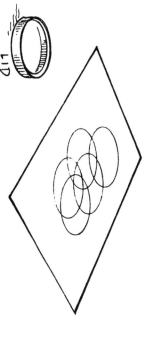

LID

RULER

PROTRACTOR

ANGLE

CRAYON

LID

PENCIL

CHALK

MARKER

TEMPLATE

HINT

• The clue to developing a creative imagination is to stand back and let the artists make their own discoveries. Let the artists explore and create, sharing their delight with different results and processes.

D
R
A
W
I
N
G

ALL ages

BASICS

Sand and Glue Drawing

Materials

sand in large, wide tub (a sand table works well)
white glue in bottles
white glue in cup with a paintbrush or cotton swab
paper, posterboard or matte board

Art Process

1. Place a sheet of paper, posterboard or matte board in the tub on the surface of the sand.
2. Draw a design on the paper with the glue from a bottle or with a paintbrush dipped in the cup of glue.
3. When the design is complete, scoop handfuls of sand from the tub and cover the entire paper with sand.
4. Pick up the paper from the corner and let the excess sand fall back into the tub.
5. Set sand drawing aside to dry.

Variations

- Fill a yogurt cup half full of sand, add some powdered tempera paint and stir the sand and paint together to make colored sand. Make several colors in different cups. Use the colored sand for drawings by sprinkling pinches and bits of sand in specific places on the design rather than an all over design as above.
- Make sand drawings on the playground or the sidewalk. Do not use any glue. Simply squeeze dry sand from a mustard squeeze bottle making lines, dots and other designs directly on the side-walk. Sweep away the sand when complete.

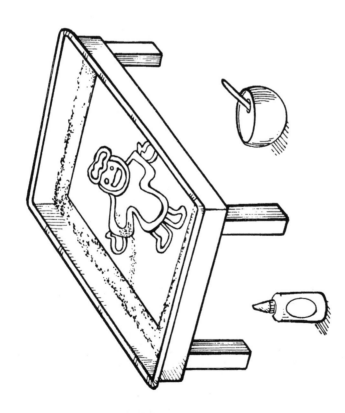

HINT
- Clean sand can be purchased from hardware stores.
- If blobs of glue-sand fall into the tub from the paper, let them dry and remove when hardened.

Ironed Wax Paper

Materials

old pieces of crayons, peeled
old cheese grater
wax paper cut into 8" x 10" (20 cm x 25 cm) pieces
newspaper
old iron set on warm
scissors
yarn, optional

Art Process

1. Work on a thick pad of newspaper.
2. Place a sheet of wax paper on the newspaper.
3. Grate crayons onto the sheet of wax paper.
4. Cover the crayon shavings and wax paper with a second sheet of wax paper.
5. Cover this with another sheet of newspaper.
6. **Adult** irons over the newspaper to melt the crayon shavings beneath and "glue" wax paper pieces together.
7. Remove the top newspaper. Trim the excess edges of the wax paper with scissors. Glue a piece of yarn to the project if the artist wishes to hang the design in a window.

Variations

- Wax paper can be used in a variety of sizes or shapes. You may choose to frame the finished project with colored paper.
- Sometimes pressing straight down with the iron and then lifting it straight up (instead of rubbing it back and forth) creates different designs in the melted crayon.

HINT

- With careful supervision the artist can do the ironing. Most children can be very careful.
- Tape the iron cord in place so artists in the room don't trip over it.
- This project should be supervised by an adult at all times.

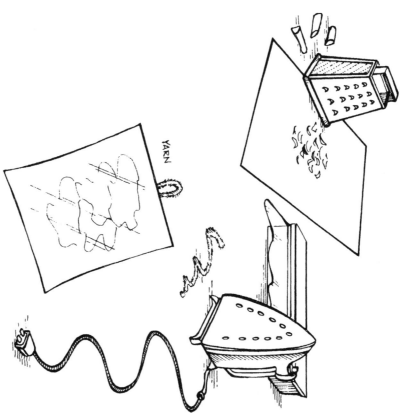

YARN

BASICS

Warm Crayon

Materials

food-warming tray, electrical (look at garage sales and in thrift stores)

paper
old crayons, peeled
oven mitt or thick glove
masking tape, optional
paper towels

Art Process

1. Turn on the warming tray to a very warm setting, but not dangerously hot.
2. Place a piece of paper on the warmed tray. An **adult** may tape the paper to the tray to hold it in place.
3. Wear a thick glove or oven mitt on the non-drawing hand. Use this hand to hold the paper still.
4. With the free drawing hand, move a crayon slowly over the heated paper and make a melted design.
5. Wipe the warming tray with a dry paper towel after each use and the warm, melted crayon wax spills will disappear quickly leaving a clean tray for the next artist.

Variations

• Cover the tray with heavy duty aluminum foil. Draw directly on the warm aluminum foil. Press a paper towel or piece of paper onto the melted design, peel the paper off and observe the design transferred to the paper. Remember to wipe the tray clean with a paper towel to remove the excess crayon design.

HINT
• Artists must be told to keep hands and arms off the warming tray.
• Tape the electric cord to the table with masking tape.
• This project should be supervised by an adult at all times.

Vegetable Dye Paint

Powdered vegetable food dye is a harmless food coloring. Although fairly expensive in small quantities, it can be bought inexpensively in bulk by the pound. One pound should last a preschool for several years and a family for generations. This material makes the best paint the author has ever used.

Materials

1/8 teaspoon powdered vegetable food dye
   (available at school supply stores)
1 tablespoon water
liquid starch
mixing cup
measuring spoons
stirring spoon

Art Process

1. Dissolve the dye powder in the water.
2. Add liquid starch to reach desired color intensity.
3. Stir the mixture.
4. Paint as with any paint.

Variations

- Food dye mixed with wallpaper paste or hobby and craft paste makes a brilliant and translucent paint.
- Food coloring is a substitute for vegetable food dye.
- To make a more intense color, use one-half teaspoon dye.

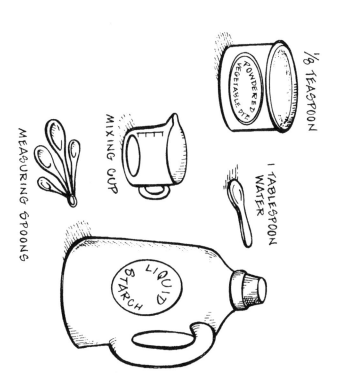

1/8 TEASPOON

1 TABLESPOON WATER

MIXING CUP

MEASURING SPOONS

STIRRING SPOON

LIQUID STARCH

HINT

- Powdered vegetable food dye is available at school supply stores in bright blue, dull blue, red, yellow and green. The powders can be mixed to make new colors such as purple, brown or orange.
- Paint from food dye is somewhat transparent.

PAINTING

BASICS

Free Paint

Materials

tempera paints with brushes
cup of water for rinsing
rag for drying
any paper
work surface such as floor, table, easel, wall or board for the lap

Art Process

1. Choose a paper and a work surface.
2. Choose a color of paint.
3. Begin painting on the paper, rinsing the brush when changing colors.
4. Paint until the design is complete. The work can be a design, a pattern or a more realistic rendering. Whatever the artist paints is acceptable.
5. Dry the work on the work surface or remove to a drying area.

Variations

- Experiment with different textures of paper, different mixtures of thick and thin tempera paint and different amounts of water used for the watercolor paints.
- Experiment with mixing colors.
- Sometimes it is interesting to alter the paper used for painting. For example, cut the paper in a variety of shapes for painting or cut out shapes from a piece of paper to be painted. Newspaper or wrapping paper can also be used as a surface for painting designs.

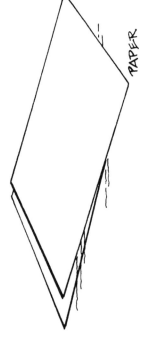

TEMPERA PAINT

TEMPERA PAINT

BRUSHES

RAG

PAPER

HINT · Free painting is simply painting on paper with no particular expectations from anyone. There is no end to the possibilities of what will emerge from free painting.

PAINTING

BASICS

Watercolor Paint

Materials
watercolor paint box and paintbrush
cup of water for rinsing
paper
rag for drying
newspaper covered work surface

Art Process
1. Dip a paintbrush in the clear water and then into one of the watercolor paint colors.
2. Paint on the paper.
3. Rinse the brush in the clear water and continue painting with the watercolor paints.
4. Change the rinse water when it gets murky.
5. Paint until the artwork is complete.
6. Dry on the work surface or move to a drying area by lifting the entire sheet of newspaper and carrying the painting on the newspaper.

Variations
- Experiment with mixing colors in the lid of the paint box or on the paper.
- Paint on wet paper.
- Outline dry designs with permanent felt pen.
- Sprinkle the paint with salt.

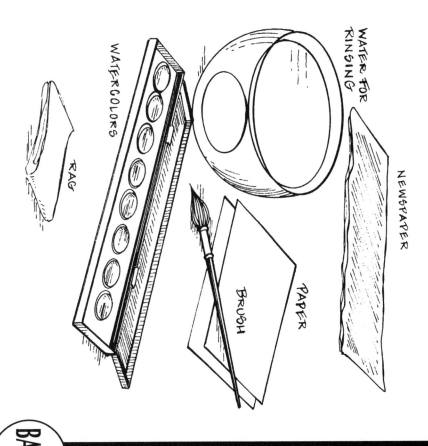

HINT
- Young artists often hold up their paintings for adults to admire. Watercolor paintings are usually dripping wet which can be a bit messy. Remind artists to hold their wet creations "flat" or call the adult to their work spot for viewing the creation.

PAINTING

BASICS

Fingerpainting

Materials

powdered or liquid tempera paint
liquid starch
big paper
newspaper
cover artist in apron or big shirt
soapy water in bucket and towel

Art Process

1. Open a full sheet of newspaper and place on the floor or table.
2. Place a large piece of paper on the newspaper.
3. Pour a puddle of liquid starch about the size of a piece of bread in the middle of the paper.
4. Place a squeeze of liquid tempera paint or a rounded spoonful of powdered tempera paint in the middle of the starch puddle.
5. Begin to smear and mix the paint and starch by hand.
6. When paint is spread across the paper, begin to fingerpaint by drawing fingers and hands through the paint. Elbows and arms make interesting designs too.
7. If paint dries out, add a bit more starch to the paper.
8. When painting is complete, lift entire sheet of newspaper with painting on it and carry to a drying area.
9. When dry, peel the finished project carefully from the newspaper. You may wish to place the artwork on a clean sheet of newspaper before drying to prevent painting from sticking to the newspaper.

SOAPY WATER

NEWSPAPER

BIG PAPER

TEMPERA PAINT

APRON

HINT · Glossy or shiny papers work the best.
· This is a messy project. Even artists who cover their clothing still seem to get paint on their clothes.

PAINTING

BASICS

Easel Painting

Materials
paint easel with clips for paper
covered easel board
large sheets of newsprint or butcher paper
paints in cups
large paintbrush for each cup
covered floor under easel
paint apron or big shirt for artist

Art Process
1. Clip a small stack of paper to the easel. (The top piece can be slipped out when painting is complete; the next piece of paper will be ready for the artist.)
2. Fill the cups with tempera paints mixed to a medium consistency that will avoid runny drips. Use cups available from school supply stores with a snap-on lids containing a hole for the brush. Yogurt cups also work well, as do small milk cartons. Both of these versions can be thrown away after using for a period of time.
3. Dip brushes into paint and paint on the paper (see hint).
4. When painting is complete, remove the painting from the easel and clip to a drying rack until dry. A fish net on the wall with clothes pins provides a good drying area.

Variation
· Place other art mediums at the easel such as chalk, watercolors, felt pens or unusual paint recipes such as Vegetable Dye Paint (see p. 27).

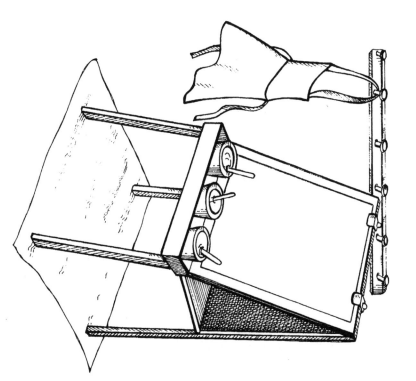

(see p. 27).

HINT
· Young artists do not have the adult concept of keeping brushes in only one color of paint or keeping cups of paint clean. Young artists are involved in painting and mixing colors. As much as adults would like the cups of paint to stay clean and unmixed with other colors, it may not happen.

ALL ages

PAINTING

BASICS

Paint Dough

Materials

flour
water
salt
liquid tempera paint
measuring cup
bowls, mixing spoons
posterboard or matte board
plastic squeeze bottles

Art Process

1. Mix equal parts of flour, salt and water to form a paste consistency.
2. Add paint to desired color. Make several different colors.
3. Pour each paint mixture into a plastic squeeze bottle.
4. Squeeze paint onto the posterboard or matte board to make designs.
5. Dry the completed project. The salt gives the designs a glistening crystal quality when dry.

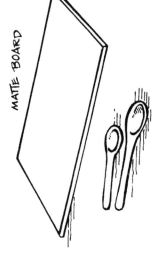

MATTE BOARD

FLOUR

WATER

SALT

TEMPERA PAINT

BOWLS

SQUEEZE BOTTLES

HINT
- Different colors of paint mixtures will not mix together when colors bump into each other. They maintain their own separate design and space, which is different from regular paints.
- Paint mixture can dry and harden in squeeze bottles so rinse bottles clean when project is complete.

ALL ages

author's favorite

Runnies

Materials

several colors of tempera paint
cups
spoons for each color
paper
masking tape, optional
cookie sheet

Art Process

1. Place a piece of paper on a cookie sheet. Tape the corners to hold the paper in place.
2. Mix several colors of tempera paint in cups to a thin consistency and place a spoon in each cup of paint.
3. Spoon one color of paint on the paper. Next, tip the cookie sheet to make the color run across the paper making tracks.
4. Now add another color. Tip the cookie sheet again. The colors will run into each other and mix.
5. Add as many colors and tip as many times as desired.
6. When finished, remove the paper from the cookie sheet and place in a drying area. You may also choose to dry the painting on the cookie sheet and remove later.

Variation

· Place a puddle of paint on the paper and blow the paint in different directions using a drinking straw. Remind the artist to blow out only so no paint will be accidently swallowed!

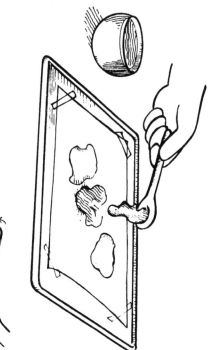

HINT
· Thick paint runs too but may need a little coaxing with a paintbrush or toothpick to get it started.
· The cookie sheet helps control spills and drips. It works best if it has sides.

Paint Blots

Materials

tempera paints in cups
spoon or paintbrush for each color
paper, pre-folded down the middle
covered work surface
scissors, optional

Art Process

1. Place the pre-folded piece of paper on the covered work surface and open it out flat.
2. Drop blobs of paint on the fold or on one side of the paper.
3. Fold over the other side of the paper and rub or press the paper very gently. Pressing outward from the fold spreads the paint out onto the paper.
4. Unfold the paper to see what the "blot" looks like.
5. Make more blots on new paper. Think about what shapes might occur and what colors might mix together.
6. Dry the completed project. Cut out the design if desired.

Variations

- Make huge blots on huge paper.
- Blots can be cut out and made into butterflies, flowers, bugs or other imaginary things.
- For the more advanced artistic thinker, attempt to make shapes such as a heart, snowflake, pumpkin or other form.

HINT · Pressing gently seems to be an important factor in making blots that appeal to artists. To test the technique, make a blot by pressing really hard. Next make another one by pressing gently. The artist can decide which technique is most suitable.

Monoprint

Materials

washable table
powdered tempera paint
liquid starch
spoon
paintbrush
paper
newspaper covered drying area

Art Process

1. Pour a puddle of liquid starch directly on the table.
2. Add a spoonful of powdered tempera paint to the puddle.
3. Mix the starch and paint with hands or a paintbrush, spreading it out on the table to a size that will fit the piece of paper.
4. Draw a design in the paint using the fingers.
5. When the design is complete, gently place the sheet of paper over the design and pat without pressing too hard.
6. Lift the paper from the design by the corner, peeling it away from the paint.
7. A monoprint of the design will be on the paper. Place the paper on some newspaper to dry.
8. Additional prints may be made from the same design or a new design can be made and printed.

Variations

- Add more than one color or paint to the puddle of starch and experiment with combinations of colors and mixing colors.
- Instead of painting on the table top, paint on a sheet of Plexiglas or on a cookie sheet.

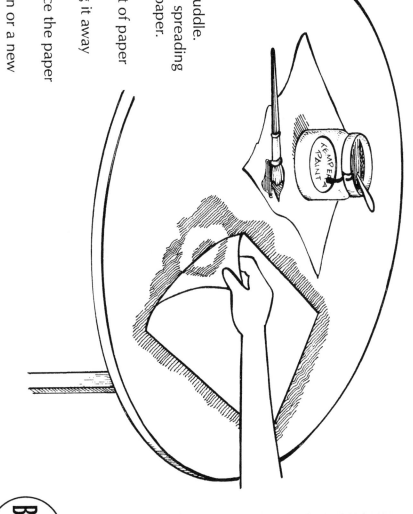

HINT
- If the paint on the table dries out, add more starch to make it smooth and ready again.
- Curled, dry paintings can be ironed to flatten.

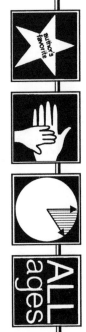

BASICS

Dip and Dye Papers

Materials

one of the following papers—coffee filters, paper towels, napkins, ink blotter or white tissue paper

covered table

sheets of newsprint

cups of food coloring or paper dye

eyedroppers

drying area

Art Process

1. Cover a table with thick layers of newspaper.
2. Place sheets of newsprint around the table like placemats where each artist will work.
3. There are several techniques in Dip and Dye. The easiest one is to first place a paper towel on the newsprint and then squeeze drops of food coloring or paper dye from an eyedropper onto the paper towel. Another technique is to fold the paper towel and then dip the corners of the towel into the cups of dye. Unfold carefully and place the towel on the sheet of newsprint. A coffee filter is perhaps the best paper to fold and dip in the cups of dye.
4. Experiment with dipping and dying any of the papers suggested.
5. Carry the wet dyed towel or paper on the sheet of newsprint to a drying area and dry for an hour or so. If dying a thin paper such as white tissue, unfold the wet dyed paper as far as possible without tearing and dry overnight. Finish unfolding the dry paper the next day. When completely dry, iron the paper with adult help if necessary.

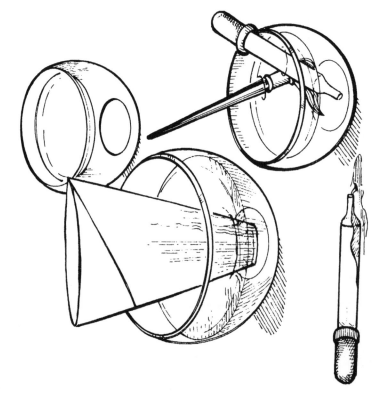

HINT
- Paper dyes are available at art stores in jars of highly concentrated powdered dyes. Although fairly expensive, the dyes will last for years and the colors are incredibly bright and vibrant. In the long run, the powdered dyes are cheaper and better than food coloring.

Basics

Paint and Print

Materials

things to use for making prints—kitchen utensils, gadgets, toys, sponges, fingertips or inflated balloons

liquid tempera paints

pan or tray

paper towels

paintbrush

paper

covered work surface

Art Process

1. Place a pad of wet paper towels in the pan or tray.
2. Spread liquid tempera paint on the paper towels for a print pad.
3. Press an object into the paint and then press it onto the paper. Press the object on the paper several times before replacing it in the paint. Random designs or patterns are two of the design possibilities.
4. Dry the design on the work surface or move the wet design to a drying area.

Variations

- Experiment printing with ink, food coloring, watercolor paints, thick and thin tempera paint or paper or fabric dye.
- Make wrapping paper, a wall hanging, greeting cards, a framed poster or simply enjoy the artwork and eventually discard.
- Wrap string around a block of wood or toilet paper tube for a string print.
- Cut cardboard shapes and glue to a block of wood for a relief print.

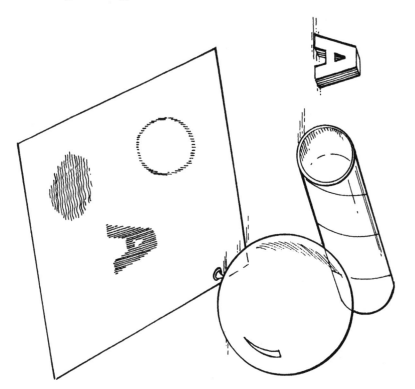

HINT · Encourage young artists to press the object gently into the paint and then onto the paper because it makes a better print. Some young minds think that the harder and louder you whack the object into the paint and then onto the paper, the more impressive the print will be.

Handy Prints (Footie, Too)

P A I N T I N G

Materials

hands and feet
tempera paints and brush
shallow tray
paper
covered work surface
bucket of soapy water and towels

Art Process

1. Pour several colors of thick tempera paints into separate trays. Three different colors work well.
2. Paint the artist's hand with a brush or press the hand into the paint.
3. The artist presses the painted hand onto the paper. Press again on the paper without repainting if desired.
4. Re-paint the hand in a new color or the same color. Continue printing on the paper. Overlap colors to make new colors.
5. Wash and dry hands before carrying the print to a drying area.
6. Make foot prints too! Follow the same procedures using the artist's foot instead of hand. Walk on long paper or make single prints on small paper.

Variations

- Make a single hand print on a paper plate.
- Use both hands, feet, elbows or the nose to make prints from other parts of the body. Have fun! This is a good project to do outside.

HINT
- A hand washing bucket or a large, shallow tub usually works better than a sink. A bucket is easy to clean and easy for the kids to use. Make sure you change the water in the bucket often if hands and feet are printing. The paint usually stains the skin but wears away in a day or two.

Rock Painting

Materials
flat rocks, any size
tempera paints in cups
medium point paintbrushes
newspaper covered work area
clear acrylic craft paint, optional

Art Process
1. Collect flat rocks at the beach, along the river or purchase from
   a landscape garden supplier.
2. This project may be completed outdoors or inside.
3. Place rocks on a work surface covered with newspaper.
4. Dip a medium point brush into tempera paint and paint a
   design on the rock.
5. If painting the underside of the rock too, let the top dry before
   turning the rock over. When dry, turn the rock over and paint
   the underside of the rock.
6. **Adult** covers the design with a clear acrylic craft paint to protect
   the design if desired.

Variations
- When the basic design is dry on the rock, use a fine point brush
  to add details.
- Use felt pens for the design or to add details to a dry painted
  rock.
- Use the finished product for paperweights, bookends or table
  decorations.
- Stack and glue rocks together to make painted rock sculptures.

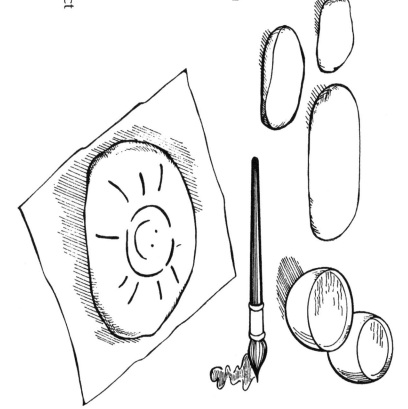

HINT · *Older children can use acrylic paints which won't
wash or smudge off the rock when dry.*

BASICS

Craft Clay

Materials

4 cups (800 g) flour
1 cup (200 g) salt
bowl
1-1/2 cups (345 ml) warm water
wooden spoon

baking sheet
cutting board
plastic wrap
foil or wax paper
oven

Art Process

1. Combine the flour and salt in a bowl.
2. Make a well in the center of the dry ingredients and pour in one cup warm water. Mix the dough with your hands.
3. Add more water and continue mixing. The dough should not be crumbly or sticky, but should form a ball.
4. Knead the dough on a floured board until smooth (about five minutes).
5. Work with a small portion of dough at a time on a piece of foil or wax paper. Keep the rest of the dough wrapped in plastic and in the refrigerator. (If it dries out, add a few drops of water and knead.) All dough parts should be joined together with water, using a brush or fingers.
6. When a sculpture or object is complete, **adult** places it on a foil covered baking sheet and bakes at 325 degrees one hour or until hard. Dough should not "give" when tapped with a knife.

Variation

· Some ideas for things to make include napkin rings; jewelry; beads; pretend rolls, bread, bagels; pretend fruits, vegetables and play foods; picture frames; bugs and insects; animals or holiday decorations.

HINT · Work directly on a baking sheet to prevent tearing or breaking the objects when moving them.

· Breaks and cracks in baked pieces can be repaired with white glue forced into the crack or fresh dough can be pressed between broken pieces, re-baked and then covered with paint.

BASICS

C
L
A
Y

ALL ages

caution

author's favorite

Yeast Dough

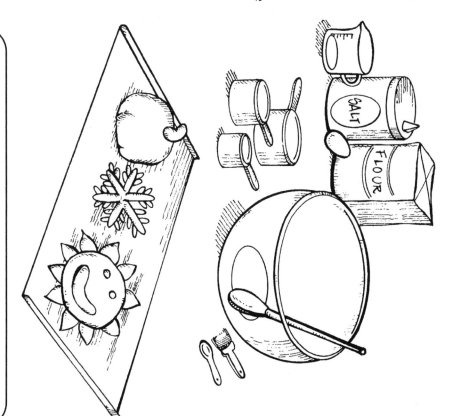

Materials

1 package yeast
1-1/2 cups (345 ml) warm water
1 teaspoon salt
1 tablespoon sugar
4 cups (800 g) flour
measuring cups and spoons

large bowl and mixing spoon
greased cookie sheet
pastry brush
1 egg, beaten
salt (optional)
oven

Art Process

1. With adult help, measure 1-1/2 cups warm water into the large bowl. Sprinkle yeast into water and stir until soft.
2. Add the salt, sugar and flour. Mix until dough forms a ball.
3. Knead on floured surface until smooth and elastic.
4. Roll and twist dough into shapes such as letters, animals and unique shapes.
5. Place the dough sculptures on a greased cookie sheet. Cover and let rise in a warm place until double in size.
6. Brush each sculpture with beaten egg. Sprinkle with salt (optional).
7. Bake for 12 to 15 minutes at 350 degrees until sculptures are firm and golden brown
8. Cool slightly. Eat and enjoy! Yum!

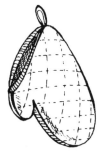

HINT

• Use this delicious dough to make healthy, seasonal treats such as jack-o-lanterns in the fall, snowflakes in the winter, bunnies in the spring and great big suns in the summer.

BASICS

C
L
A
Y

Playful Clay

Materials

measuring cups
pan
1 cup (200 g) baking soda
1/2 cup (100 g) cornstarch
2/3 cup (150 g) warm water
stove
cutting board
food coloring or tempera paints
newspaper
clear nail polish, optional

Art Process

1. Mix baking soda and cornstarch in a pan.
2. Add water and stir until smooth.
3. **Adult** places the pan over medium heat. Boil and stir until the consistency of mashed potatoes. Pour the mixture onto the cutting board to cool.
4. Knead the dough when cool.
5. For color, knead food coloring into clay until blended. Objects may also be painted when completely dry.
6. Explore and create with the Playful Clay.
7. When objects are complete, harden or dry on newspaper for several hours.
8. For a shine, **adult** paints the dry objects with clear nail polish.

Variation

- Crush colored chalk and knead into the dough for a speckled coloring.

HINT

- *This recipe makes one and one-half cups of dough. It can be doubled easily.*
- *The dough stores in an airtight container for several weeks but will dry out if exposed to the air.*
- *This material hardens quickly.*

BASICS

Cooked Playdough

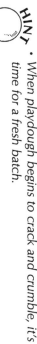

Materials

measuring cups and spoons
1 cup (200 g) flour
1 cup (200 g) salt
1 cup (230 ml) water
1 tablespoon cream of tartar
food coloring
pan
stove
spoon
cutting board
cooking utensils for sculpting and play
plastic container with lid for storage

Art Process

1. With an adult, mix the flour, water, salt and cream of tartar in a pan. (For colored dough, add food coloring to the water and mix with the other ingredients.)
2. **Adult** places the pan over low heat and stirs until the dough forms a ball.
3. Remove the pan from the heat, pour the ball on a cutting board and knead until smooth and pliable.
4. Give the warm dough to the artist to begin sculpting, exploring, playing and creating. Provide any variety of utensils and tools for exploration such as a rolling pin or wooden dowel, cookie cutters, a fork, nuts and bolts or a garlic press.
5. The dough can be stored in a plastic container for a week or so.

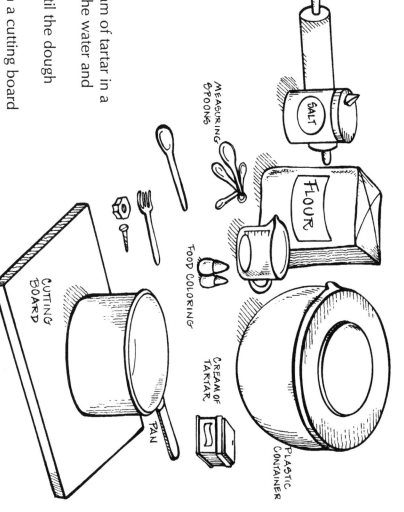

MEASURING SPOONS
SALT
FLOUR
FOOD COLORING
CREAM OF TARTAR
PLASTIC CONTAINER
CUTTING BOARD
PAN

HINT
· When playdough begins to crack and crumble, it's time for a fresh batch.
· Double this recipe for twice as much fun.

BASICS

caution

ALL ages

No-Cook Playdough

Materials

measuring cups and spoons
1 cup (230 ml) cold water
1 cup (200 g) salt
2 teaspoons oil
3 cups (600 g) flour
2 tablespoons cornstarch
powdered paint or food coloring
bowl and spoon
cutting board

Art Process

1. In a bowl mix the water, salt, oil and enough powdered paint to make a bright color. Dough can also be left white.
2. Gradually work flour and cornstarch into the mixture until it reaches a bread dough consistency.
3. Pour the dough on a cutting board and knead.
4. Use this dough to model as with any clay.

Variation

• Color the dough with food coloring or paste coloring.

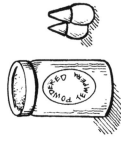

HINT • *This quick and easy clay does not dry well but is a pliable, bright and colorful modeling clay.*

BASICS

Great Goop

Materials

one part cornstarch
one part water
plastic tub or large baking pan
large measuring cup
other measuring cups
spoon
food coloring, optional

Art Process

1. Mix the cornstarch with water in a large measuring cup. With one cup of cornstarch, use one cup of water. With four cups of cornstarch, use four cups of water and so on.
2. Add food coloring if desired. It is not necessary.
3. Pour the mixture into a tub or large baking pan.
4. Begin to experience and enjoy this mixture's unique properties and surprises.

Variations

· Add more cornstarch or more water and see what happens to the mixture.
· Make Great Goop in a water table or large tub for a group experience. Add utensils such as a spatula, rolling pin or whisk to manipulate the mixture.

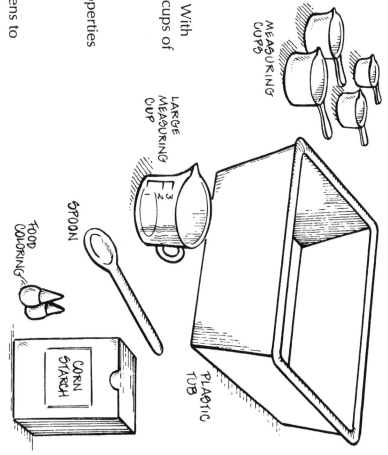

MEASURING CUPS

LARGE MEASURING CUP

SPOON

FOOD COLORING

CORN STARCH

PLASTIC TUB

HINT

· Do not pour the Great Goop down the sink when exploring is complete. Scoop it into a paper or plastic bag and discard in the trash.

· This is a very messy but wonderful project! Have a hand washing bucket nearby for easy cleanup.

BASICS

C
L
A
Y

Peanut Butter Dough

Materials

measuring cups and spoons
1 part peanut butter
1 part non-fat dry milk (powdered milk)
1 tablespoon honey per cup, optional
bowl
spatula
kneading surface
covered container

Art Process

1. Wash and dry hands before beginning this edible dough.
2. Mix equal parts of peanut butter and dry milk together in a bowl by hand.
3. Add honey if desired.
4. Knead and mix the dough until it has a stiff, dough-like consistency.
5. Model and experiment with the peanut butter dough like any playdough.
6. Eat and enjoy your art creation!

Variation

- Add other ingredients such as raisins, shredded coconut, chocolate chips or bits of dry breakfast cereal into the dough or use to decorate the dough designs.

POWDERED MILK

PEANUT BUTTER

MEASURING CUP

BOWL

HONEY

SPATULA

COVERED CONTAINER

HINT
- One cup of peanut butter and one cup of dry milk makes a nice ball of dough for one child.
- This dough models fairly well but does not harden.
- This dough keeps well in a covered container in the refrigerator.

BASICS

D O U G H

Soap Clay

Materials

2 cups (400 g) white detergent flakes (such as Ivory Snow)
2 tablespoons water
food coloring, optional
bowl

Art Process

1. Pour detergent in a bowl.
2. Add water or colored water gradually while mixing and squeezing with hands until soap forms a ball.
3. Add more water if necessary.
4. Model and explore Soap Clay, squeezing and forming different shapes.
5. Clean-up is easy with warm water and a towel handy. Hands are already soapy!

Variations

· Make soap balls to use at home or school.
· Give soap balls or soap shapes as gifts.
· Mix natural materials into Soap Clay such as oatmeal or crushed dried flower petals.
· Add fragrance to the Soap Clay with spices such as cinnamon or with extracts such as almond or lemon.
· Try carving the Soap Clay with a spoon, toothpick or other tool.

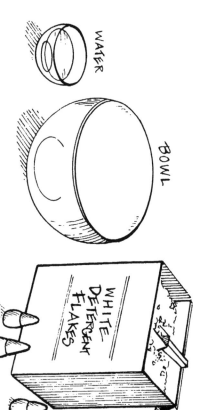

WATER

BOWL

WHITE DETERGENT FLAKES

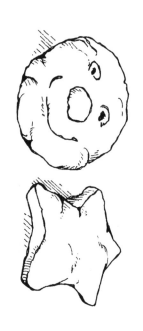

HINT
· Once in a while someone will put a soapy finger in his or her mouth. The adult should calmly provide clear water and a cup at the sink. Keep rinsing out the mouth until the taste is gone. If someone gets soap in his or her eye, flood the eye with clear water until the stinging is gone.

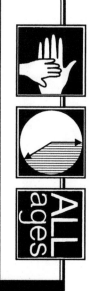

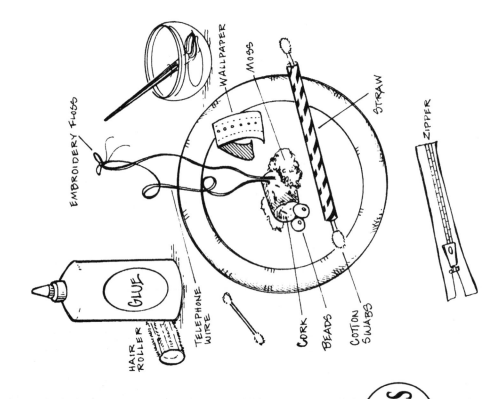

Collage

ALL ages · author's favorite

Materials

any collage items (see suggestions below)
white glue in a squeeze bottle or white glue thinned with water in a cup with a paintbrush
materials for a base such as paper, wood, cardboard, an old file folder, matte board, a paper plate, a styrofoam tray or box

Art Process

1. Using glue, stick any collage items to a chosen base.
2. Any design and any amount or type of collage items makes each collage unique.
3. Dry the project completely, sometimes overnight, if the glue is very thick.

Variations

· A group can work on a collage together with everyone participating on a large base.
· Choose a theme for a collage such as shapes, colors, plants, happiness, good foods or textures.
· The following is a small list of collage suggestions: acorns, bark, beads, bobby pins, bolts, bones, bottle caps, cellophane, confetti, cork, cotton swabs, eggshells, embroidery thread, fabric, feathers, felt, flowers, foil gift wrap, glitter, hair rollers, hooks, ice cream sticks, inner tube scraps, jewelry, keys, lace, meat trays, moss, newspapers, origami paper, paper dots, pebbles, pine cones, ribbons, rocks, sawdust, shells, stars, sticks, string, telephone wire, tiles, toothpicks, vermiculite, wallpaper, wood scraps, wood shavings, wooden beads, yarn or zippers.

C O L L A G E

BASICS

Tissue Collage

Materials

art tissue paper in a variety of colors
scissors
tray
liquid starch in a cup
paintbrush
white paper, matte board or paper plate

Art Process

1. Cut several colors of art tissue paper into squares, triangles, rectangles or any shapes from one to three inches in size. Place the shapes on a tray.
2. Dip a paintbrush into liquid starch and brush it on the paper, matte board or paper plate.
3. Press a piece of tissue into the starch.
4. Paint a little more starch over the tissue paper.
5. Continue adding more and more pieces of tissue paper and starch, overlapping them to create new colors.
6. The artist may choose to cover all or part of the background.
7. Dry the project completely.

Variations

- Work on wax paper, plastic wrap or any variety of background papers.
- Use clear contact paper and stick the art tissue pieces to the sticky side of the contact paper. Then cover the artwork with another piece of contact paper. No starch is needed.
- Substitute thinned white glue with starch for a stronger and glossier creation.

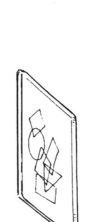

HINT

- When the tissue pieces are painted with starch the color or dye runs out of the paper. Although this is a pretty effect, it can also surprise some artists.
- Keep both a wet rag and a dry rag handy to clean up sticky fingers.

ALL ages

C
O
L
L
A
G
E

BASICS

Cut and Paste

ALL ages

Materials

scraps of a variety of papers such as colored paper, wallpaper, tissue paper or magazine pages

any pastes or glues

scissors

sheets of paper for background

Art Process

1. Using scissors, cut scraps of paper in any desired shape or design.
2. Paste or glue the shape to a larger sheet of paper.
3. Continue cutting and pasting. Designs can be random or realistic.
4. Tearing paper into shapes is an alternate technique to use.
5. The design should dry in a few hours or less.

Variations

- Create a three dimensional structure, sculpture or construction with paper and paste.
- Make a theme Cut and Paste such as Colors I Love, Wallpapers Only, My Happy Design or Holiday Paste-up.
- Add other collage items to the cut and paste project.

TISSUE PAPER

LACE

GLUE

PASTE

NEWSPAPER DESIGN

MAGAZINE PAGE

WALLPAPER

HINT · This activity provides valuable opportunities for developing creativity and skill-building in young children.

Stick-On Stick-Upon

Materials

lots of glue in bottles or in cups with paintbrushes
masking tape
clear tape
stapler
stickers
stick-on labels
collage items such as paper scraps, sewing scraps, glitter, shredded
    paper, yarn or flowers
background or base materials such as cardboard boxes, plastic
    jugs, a large ice cream container, newspaper, old
    posters or paper

Art Process

1. Choose a background or base material.
2. Begin gluing and sticking collage items such as cut-up scraps of
   paper on the base. Completely cover if desired.
3. Dry the project completely.

Variations

- Stick things on a long piece of heavy yarn or rope to make a
  wild and crazy garland to drape around a room.
- Stick things on yourself!
- Make a collage on a cardboard box or plastic jug.
- Save a variety of stick-ons and stick-upons because this activity
  can be repeated over and over with different and unique results
  each time.

HINT · Limit the variety of stickons provided the first few
times the artist explores this activity; young artists
sometimes get confused with too many choices. Bring
out more materials as the artists develop comfort with
the creativity and skill of sticking things together.

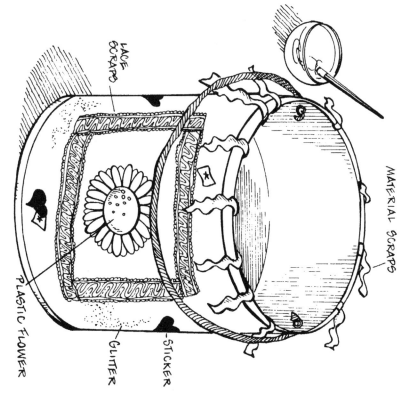

LACE SCRAPS

MATERIAL SCRAPS

PLASTIC FLOWER

GLITTER

STICKER

Lace and Sew

Materials

matte board or cardboard cut in squares

scissors and hole punch

pre-cut lengths of colored yarn (about 2' – 70 cm – long)

masking tape

Art Process 1—Lace and Wrap

1. Cut slits around the edge of a cardboard or matte board square. Adult help may be needed.
2. Pull the end of a string of yarn through a slit and then wrap the yarn through another slit, crisscrossing or wrapping the cardboard square as desired.
3. Finish the lacing by tucking the end of yarn through a slit and trimming.

Art Process 2—"Needleless" Sewing

1. Punch holes around the edge of a piece of cardboard or a styrofoam tray. Adult help may be needed.
2. Tape the end of a piece of yarn with enough masking tape to secure the end of yarn and make a needle-like end.
3. Push the taped end of the yarn through a hole, pull through and then push the yarn through the next hole. Continue "sewing" with the yarn until it runs out. Tape the end down.
4. You may sew with more yarn if you wish.

Variations

- Color in the shapes between the yarn with felt pens.
- Use embroidery thread instead of yarn.
- Sew on old greeting cards.

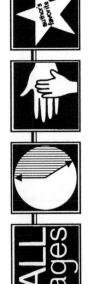

HINT
- Keep the yarn no longer than two feet in length.
- If using one of the large plastic darning needles, thread the needle with a doubled four foot length of yarn, tie both ends in a knot and begin sewing.
- Allow space between artists so no one get poked.

Wood Sculpture

Materials

scraps of wood (see hints below)

matte board cardboard or square of wood for base, optional

white glue

decorating items such as tempera paint, glitter, confetti, ribbon, nails, felt pens, nuts and bolts, pieces of straws, pieces of old toys, rubber bands or bits of collage materials

Art Process

1. Collect scraps of wood from a high school shop class or a picture frame shop. Wood shop classes using jig-saws can save curved, puzzle-like and unusually shaped pieces that are creative treasures when making wood sculptures.
2. Work on a base of matte board or a square of wood if desired.
3. Glue pieces of scrap wood together much like building with blocks. (For quicker and stronger sculptures, an adult can handle a glue gun for the artist. This technique must be supervised closely.)
4. Let the sculpture dry overnight.
5. When dry, the artist may choose to decorate or paint the sculpture.

Variations

· Build a specific object such as a house, bridge or car.
· Combine several sculptures with identical bases to make a large sculpture. Sculptures can be displayed on a wall.

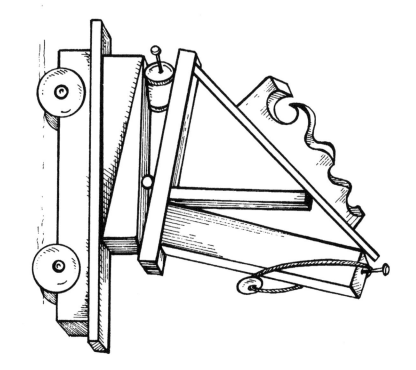

HINT
· If a sculpture is top heavy or unbalanced, white glue won't hold well. Add some masking tape, rubber bands or other supports until the glue has set. Remove the supports when the project is completely dry.

BASICS

Junk Sculpture

Materials

all kinds of recycled, reusable "junk," such as paper tubes, egg cartons, pieces of toys, bits of fabric and ribbon, corks, buttons, spools, wood scraps, foil or cardboard boxes!

white glue

something for a base, such as matte board, cardboard, heavy paper or a styrofoam tray

tempera paints and brushes, optional

Art Process

1. Glue items together to make a three-dimensional sculpture. Sculptures can be tall, short, wide or tiny but should come up off the base and have dimension.
2. When the sculpture is dry, other decorations or paints can be added.

Variations

· Choose one type of junk and make a sculpture such as a paper tube sculpture, egg carton sculpture, rocks and sticks sculpture or a wood scrap sculpture.

· Create a theme sculpture, such as Playground Trash Sculpture, Walk in the Woods Sculpture, Broken Toys Sculpture or a Happiness Sculpture.

FOIL SCRAPS

STRAWS

STICK

SPOOL

PAINTED DESIGN

BUTTONS

RIBBON

PAPER TOWEL TUBE

SHOE BOX

HINT
· Save lots and lots of interesting "junk" and this sculpture activity can be repeated over and over without the same results!

· As always, a glue-gun is an alternative for sturdy quick gluing, but requires one-on-one adult supervision.

CONSTRUCTION

BASICS

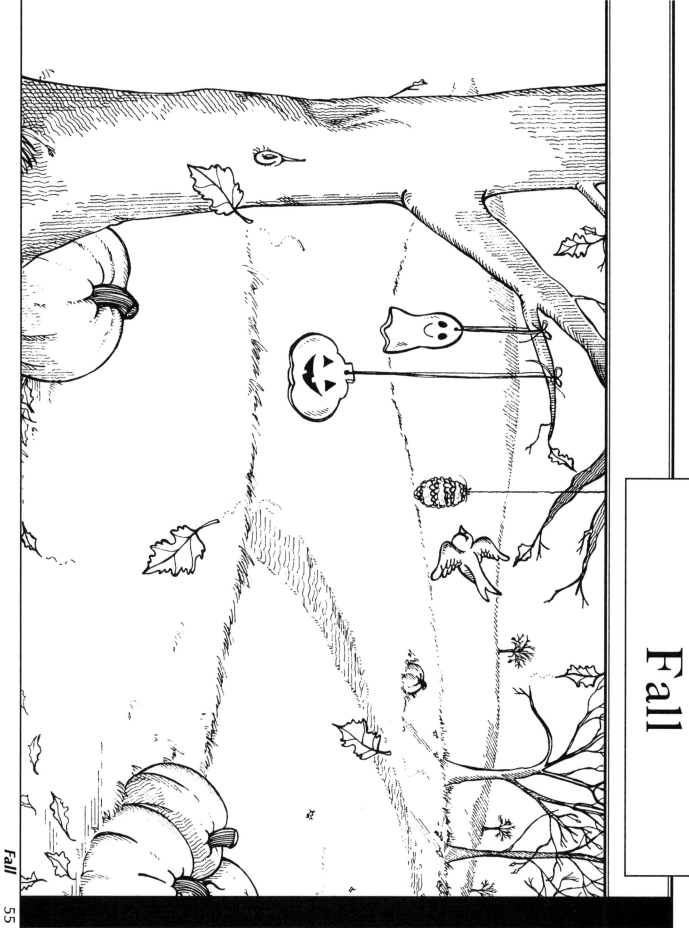

Fall

Fried Paper Plates

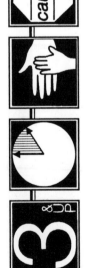

Materials

electric skillet completely lined with aluminum foil
paper plates
old crayon stubs, peeled
old cheese grater
wooden craft stick
newspaper to cover work surface
oven mitts

Art Process

1. **Adult** plugs in and turns on the electric skillet to 150 degrees or warm setting.
2. Slip a paper plate into the warm skillet.
3. Wear oven mitts to protect hands. Drop bits of old crayon stubs onto the plate.
4. Add shaved bits of crayon to the plate.
5. Push some of the crayon around with the end of a wooden craft stick to enhance the design.
6. **Adult** removes the plate from the skillet when the melted design is complete.

Variation

- Use a warming tray instead of an electric skillet to melt the crayon.

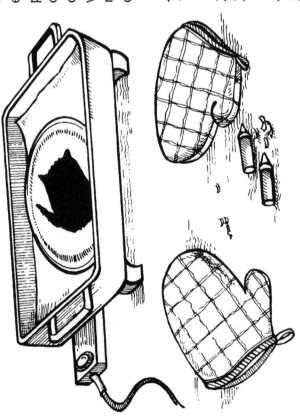

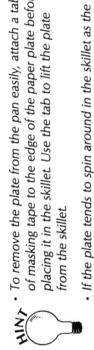

HINT
- To remove the plate from the pan easily, attach a tab of masking tape to the edge of the paper plate before placing it in the skillet. Use the tab to lift the plate from the skillet.
- If the plate tends to spin around in the skillet as the artist is working, place a loop of masking tape on the back of the paper plate before placing it in the skillet.

Baby Oil Drawing

Materials

bond paper, any color
cotton balls, cotton swabs or a paintbrush
baby oil in small dish
newspaper covered table

Art Process

1. Dip the cotton ball into the dish of baby oil.
2. Draw a design on the paper with the oil soaked cotton ball.
3. Dip other drawing tools such as a cotton swab or a paintbrush into the oil and draw on the paper.
4. After the oil soaks into the paper, hold the drawing up to the light and look at the transparent design.

Variations

· Use watercolors to paint a design on the baby oil drawing and observe how the oil resists the paint.
· Use crayons to draw on the paper and then rub the drawing with baby oil on a cotton ball to enrich the colors.

 HINT

· To prevent tipping dishes of oil during use, stick a loop of wide masking tape to the bottom of the dish, and press dish to table surface.
· Each drawing may take many cotton balls to complete since many young artists are apt to explore the delightful qualities of the soft, oily cotton ball.

3
pg.8

D
R
A
W
I
N
G

Glossy Pen Paper

Materials

heavy, glossy paper (available from scrap bin in print shops)

felt pens

paintbrush and cup of water, optional

Art Process

1. Visit a print shop and collect heavy, glossy paper used to print posters and color brochures.
2. Draw on the paper with felt pens, feeling the pens slide as the colors glide about.
3. If desired, dip a paintbrush into clear water and smudge and blur the pen marks like "paint-with-water."

Variations

- First dampen the paper with a sponge and then draw with felt pens on the wet, glossy paper.
- Experiment with felt pens on other unusual types of paper.

HINT · Ask a local printer to save a box of papers in all colors, textures and sizes. Printers are valuable sources for free and unusual paper for children, parents or teachers.

DRAWING

Fabric Pen Stencil

Materials

small squares of clear contact paper
white cotton fabric such as a shirt, sheet, pillowcase or tablecloth
fabric pens (available at fabric stores)
scissors
masking tape

Art Process

1. Spread the fabric out on the table. Tape down corners to keep fabric from slipping.
2. Cut shapes or designs from the clear contact paper.
3. Peel the backing from each shape or design and press onto the fabric.
4. Draw, color, trace or scribble over the fabric and the clear contact paper shapes. Work until the design is complete.
5. Peel the contact paper off the fabric. White areas will appear where the contact paper used to be.

Variations

- Cut letters and spell names or greetings on the fabric.
- Make planned designs and patterns for your project.
- Cut out a stencil for a design, and use the hole left from the cutout for an opposite design.
- Stick pieces of tape to heavy paper, color over them and then remove the tape.

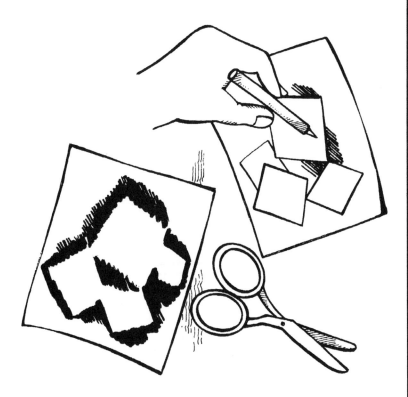

HINT
- Although kids can peel the backing of the contact paper pretty well, they sometimes need help controlling the sticky unruliness of the contact paper.
- Have some small scraps of fabric and pieces of contact paper available to practice the concept of coloring over a stencil on fabric before using the shirt or pillow case.

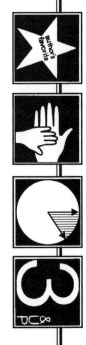

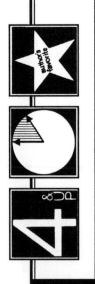

Textured Table

Materials

table

large sheet of butcher paper in any light color

peeled jumbo crayon

items to provide textures, such as yarn, sandpaper, paper shapes, fabric scraps, coins, confetti, glitter, or paper clips

masking tape

Art Process

1. Spread a variety of the texture items all around the surface of a table. These items should be fairly flat and not too pointy or sharp.

2. Place a large sheet of butcher paper over the table like a table-cloth. Tape the corners and sides of the paper to the table to prevent slipping.

3. Rub the jumbo peeled crayons on their sides back and forth all over the butcher paper. Many surprise textures will appear.

4. Feel the top of the paper with hands to be sure all the textures have been rubbed with crayon.

5. Leave the textured design on the table for a fancy table cover-ing or remove it for a wall decoration, wrapping paper or other decorative use.

Variation

• Make small rubbings on a tray with one sheet of paper. It's fun to hide items under the paper and have a friend do the rubbing to discover what is hidden beneath the paper.

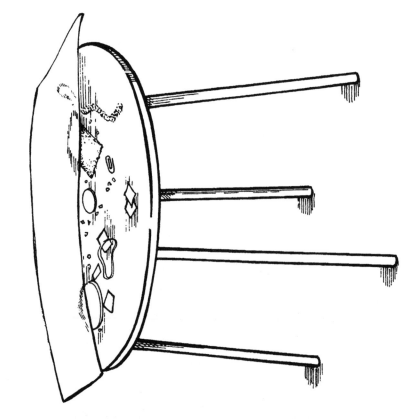

HINT · Some young artists are only beginning to understand the concept of crayon rubbings, using the sides of the crayons or finding hidden textures. This activity gives them a chance to experience rubbings with large arm movements and stable paper.

D R A W I N G

Fingerpaint Leaves

Materials
big, fall leaves
fingerpaint in containers
big paper or newsprint
newspaper covered work surface
soapy water in bucket for clean-up
towel

Art Process
1. Collect big, fall leaves (such as maple leaves) that are still supple.
2. Place a leaf on the newspaper.
3. Dip fingers in the fingerpaint and smooth and smear paint all over one side of the leaf.
4. Use fingers to draw designs into the paint on the leaf.
5. Wash and dry hands.
6. Place a sheet of newsprint over the leaf and with gentle pressure, pat the paper onto the painted leaf.
7. Peel the paper away from the leaf or peel the leaf off of the paper.
8. An imprint from the fingerpainting and the leaf will be transferred to the paper.

Variation
- Place leaves under paper and rub with peeled crayons to create leaf rubbings.

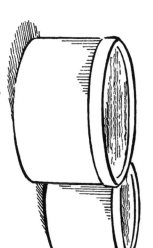

HINT • A simple fingerpaint recipe is to mix a quarter cup of liquid starch and a tablespoon of powdered or liquid tempera paint. Stir with a stick and use as fingerpaint. The measurements are not strict so experiment with color, intensity and thickness.

PAINTING

Rolling Pattern

Materials
cardboard
fresh leaves
white glue
tempera paint
cookie sheet
brayer, print roller, child's rolling pin or dowel
absorbent paper
spoon

Art Process
1. Arrange the leaves in a design on the cardboard.
2. Glue the leaves to the cardboard and let dry.
3. Place a spoonful of paint on a cookie sheet. Move the print roller or brayer through the paint until the roller is evenly coated.
4. Roll the paint on the leaves.
5. Place a piece of paper on top of the leaves.
6. Rub the paper with clean, dry hands.
7. Peel off the paper and see the raised veins and edges of the leaves imprinted on the paper.
8. Make several prints from the same painting.

Variations
- The same technique can be used with wire mesh, lace or netting instead of leaves.
- Different colors of paint can be mixed on the cookie sheet for a swirl of colors on the leaves.

HINT
- Moist, fresh leaves work the best.
- Brayers are art rollers and are available at art supply stores and school supply stores.

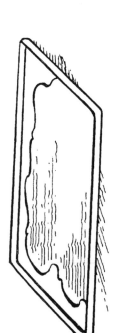

PAINTING

Scratchfoam Print

Materials

scratchfoam, cut into quarters (comes in 9" x 12" from art store) or

styrofoam grocery tray (sides trimmed away)

tempera paint on a cookie sheet

pencil

brayer (roller) or child's rolling pin

typing paper

covered work surface

Art Process

1. Press a pencil firmly into the scratchfoam to make a design (see hints).

2. Roll a brayer through the paint on the cookie sheet. Roll the brayer across the scratchfoam design.

3. Place a piece of paper on top of the scratchfoam and use gentle pressure with the fingers to deliver an even printing.

4. Peel away the paper. Dry the painting.

5. Use the same color, a new color or several new colors of paint to make another print. Re-paint the scratchfoam each time a print is made.

Variation

- Make several prints of the same design using several different colors of paper. Cut the papers in strips, reassemble the design using different colored strips and glue onto a background paper.

HINT

- Any lines or shapes pressed into the scratchfoam will show as white on the white paper; all the raised areas of the scratchfoam will print the color of the paint being used. Some artists like to think of leaving the design "tall" and the background pushed down. This is a more abstract, advanced print but many children understand it perfectly.

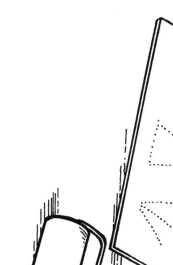

Sponge Wrap

Materials

sponges
scissors
several colors of paste food coloring mixed with a little water on a
    styrofoam grocery tray
sheets of white tissue paper
paintbrush

Art Process

1. **Adult** helps cut sponges into fall shapes such as leaves, apples, pears or pumpkins.
2. Place thinned paste food colorings in grocery trays. Keep a paintbrush handy to dab on sponges for more coverage.
3. Dip a sponge into the coloring and then press it onto an open sheet of white tissue paper. The sponge will tend to stick and lift the paper so carefully pull the sponge and paper apart.
4. Dip other sponges into the colorings, watching to see the different designs left from different shapes.
5. Print with sponges until the paper is filled with a desired design.
6. Dry the tissue paper completely. Fold and save the paper or use immediately for wrapping paper.

Variation

- Print with other items such as cork, parts of toys, blocks or cookie cutters.

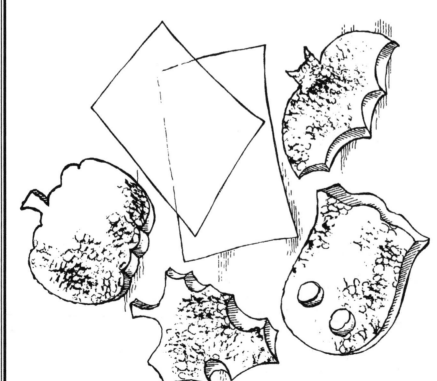

HINT
- *If wrapping paper gets wet later, the design can rub off on clothing or hands so try to keep it dry. For "stain-proof" coloring, buy fabric or paper dye from an art store. It is slightly expensive, but it goes farther, comes in a larger variety of colors and lasts longer than paste food coloring.*

PAINTING

Chalky Leaf Spatter

Materials

nail brush
wire screen, stapled to old picture frame
thin tempera paint in a bowl
chalk
paper
pressed leaves, flowers or any flat items
large cardboard box with one side cut out
tape
smock or old shirt

Art Process

1. Place a sheet of paper inside the box and tape the edges down so it won't wiggle.
2. Place leaves, flowers, grasses or paper shapes on the paper.
3. Place the wire screen in the frame over the paper. The screen should be several inches above the paper.
4. Dip the nail brush into the paint.
5. Rub the paint-filled brush many times across the screen. If the brush is loaded with paint, the spatter drops will be big and coarse.
6. Next take a piece of chalk and rub it across the screen. Bits of chalk will fall through the screen and land in the wet paint adding additional color to the spatter design. If the screen gets clogged with paint, rinse it clean, shake it dry and then add the chalk.
7. Dry the completed artwork. Remove the leaves and other objects or stencils.

HINT · The box keeps the splattering paint within a boundary. Be sure to cover the child with an old shirt too.

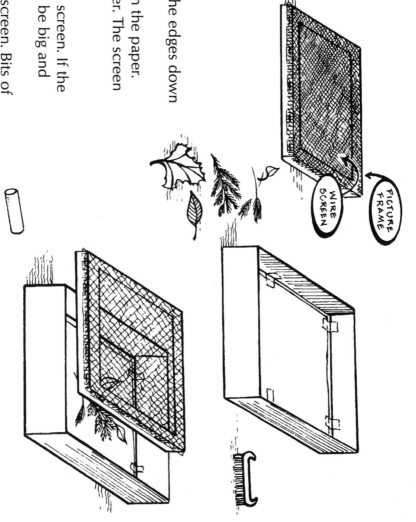

Nature Garden

Materials
playdough
heavy paper plate
fall seeds and weeds such as twigs, nuts, thistles, pine cones, seed pods, leaves, rocks, fresh or dry flowers

Art Process
1. Place a ball of playdough in the center of the paper plate. Spread the playdough out to the sides. Add more playdough to fill the plate completely with a thick layer.
2. Stick leaves, flowers and other found objects from outdoors into the playdough to make a "garden." Some leaves or weeds can also lie flat in the playdough.
3. When the design is complete, place it in the center of a table or on a shelf to enjoy.

Variations
- Make a miniature garden in an egg carton cup or a small paper plate.
- Add small figures or toys to the garden.
- Add a small mirror to the garden and partially bury it with play-dough to simulate a pond.

HINT · Collect and save things all year long for the Nature Garden.

Paper Bag Sculpture

Materials

paper bags, any size
newspaper for stuffing
strips of newspaper
wheat paste from hardware store in bowl (or make a homemade paste from recipe below)
tempera paints in cups
paintbrushes
covered work area
homemade paste for papier-mache:
Stir one and one-half cups of flour into three cups of cold water in a pan. Cook the mixture over low heat until it thickens and has a creamy paste-like consistency. Add more water if it is too thick. Cool the paste and add a few drops of peppermint oil. Use the paste to coat strips of paper.

Art Process

1. Fill a paper bag with wads of newspaper and shape the bag into any form for the base of the sculpture.
2. Dip strips of newspaper into papier-mache paste and wrap around the paper bag base. Continue using the strips to form details for the sculpture such as arms, tail or handles.
3. Squeeze the paste from each strip before placing it on the sculpture. Young artists like to pull the strip between their fingers to wring out excess paste.
4. Dry the sculpture overnight. In moist weather complete drying can take up to two days.
5. When completely dry, paint the sculpture with tempera paints.

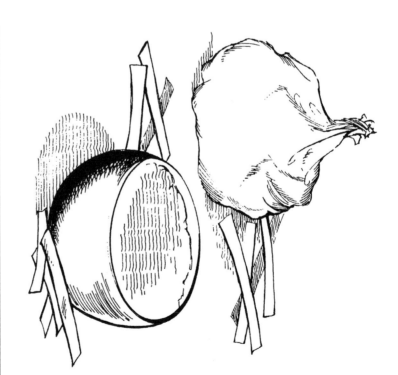

HINT

- Paper bags are easier than balloons for young children to control during their first attempt at papier-mache. Keep in mind that almost anything can be covered with papier-mache including a cardboard box, milk carton or meat tray.

- Wheat paste and wall paper paste work equally well and can be purchased in bulk containers at a hardware store.

Nature Collage

Materials

white glue

styrofoam grocery tray

nature items such as pebbles, bark, leaves, nuts, pine needles, pine cones, seeds, wood shavings, shells, seed pods or dried weeds

piece of wood for base

craft stick

cotton swab

Art Process

1. Squeeze a puddle of glue in the middle of a styrofoam grocery tray.
2. Select an item from nature and arrange it on the base piece of wood. Dab the item with glue from a craft stick or cotton swab. The artist may also choose to dip the item in the puddle of glue.
3. Now stick the item on the base piece of wood.
4. Add more bits of things from nature and attach them to the piece of wood with glue.
5. When satisfied with the arrangement, allow the collage to dry overnight or several days.

Variations

• Using felt pen or paint, make areas of color on the wood base and then glue the nature items into the color design.
• Nature Collage can be made on fabric-covered wood, a paper plate, cardboard, plaster of Paris in a pie plate or any number of other backgrounds.

HINT • As an alternative to white glue, a glue gun provides immediate, strong, long lasting results. Constant one-one-one adult supervision is necessary when using a glue gun.

Mixed-Up Magazine

Materials

pre-cut magazine pictures
paper, cardboard, box lid or paper plate for the base
paste or glue
pens or crayons

Art Process

1. Choose a magazine picture.
2. Cut an important part from the picture such as the head of a dog, a baby's foot or a glass of milk. Glue it to the base of the paper or cardboard.
3. Choose another unrelated magazine picture and add a part of that picture to the first part. The idea is to make a silly picture combining unrelated parts such as the head of a dog, the body of a boy, two feet made of bananas and so on.
4. When a substantially silly picture is complete, dry for an hour or so.

Variations

• Glue a part from a magazine picture on a piece of paper. Give the artist the challenge of adding other parts to the pre-glued piece.
• Be creative. Imagine a spaghetti face for a boy with a tree trunk body sleeping on a bed of clouds. Imagine other ideas while flipping through magazines collecting pictures.

HINT • Young artists find Mixed-Up Magazine incredibly funny. Be prepared for some very silly artists who may not want to complete one full picture but make many silly scenes. This project is truly enjoyable.

C
O
L
A
G
E

Glue Over

Materials

styrofoam grocery tray
scissors
felt pens
paintbrush
white glue in a cup

Art Process

1. **Adult** cuts a shape or piece from a styrofoam meat tray.
2. Draw on the styrofoam piece with felt pens using a wide variety of colors, completely covering the surface.
3. Dry the artwork.
4. Paint white glue over the entire surface of the colored piece.
5. Dry the glue completely to produce a slick sealed surface that brightens and enhances the colors underneath.

Variations

• Use the Glue Over as an ornament, to hang from a mobile or as a piece of artwork to hang on the wall.
• If hanging the Glue Over on the wall, use a pencil to poke a small hole in the styrofoam and insert a bit of yarn. You may also tape a paper clip to the back of the design for use as a hanger.

HINT · Glue Overs can be made very small or very large depending on the artist's choice, plan or desire.

C
R
A
F
T

Branch Weaving

Materials

tree branch with at least three smaller branches shooting out
yarn in many colors and textures
wool
nature items such as long grasses, weeds, feathers or corn husks
strips of fabric, ribbon and other strings or cords
scissors

Art Process

1. **Adult** helps the artist start at the top or the bottom of one small branch by looping some yarn around the branch to get the project started.
2. Wrap yarn around smaller branches to make a base of yarn moving up or down the branches.
3. Weave other yarn, wool, grasses, fabric strips or any intriguing items into the yarn base. Random weaving and wrapping is also effective.
4. Wrap and weave until the branch weaving is complete.

Variation

· Nail or glue strips of thin wood into a frame or box shape. Wrap and weave yarns on the wood base.

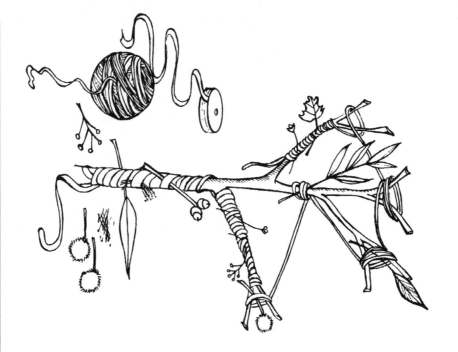

HINT · Keep the yarn about two feet in length so it doesn't get out of control. When the yarn is too long it can be frustrating and when it is too long it gets tangled. More yarn can always be added as each piece is used up.

Puzzle Paste

Materials

magazine picture or child's drawing

scissors

tag board, posterboard or heavy paper larger than the picture

glue

Art Process

1. Choose a magazine picture or a child's drawing for the puzzle picture.
2. Cut the picture or drawing into large simple shapes or strips.
3. Place the pieces of the picture on the tag board in the same order as the original picture.
4. Pick up one piece, put glue on the back and glue it to the tag board.
5. The second piece should be glued in order, but leave a space between pieces. Continue gluing the pieces to the tag board remembering to leave spaces between each piece
6. When all the pieces are glued in place, the picture will be spread out and appear to be an optical illusion because of the spaces.
7. Dry the picture for an hour.

Variation

- Glue the full, uncut picture to the tag board. When dry, take scissors and cut it into strips or large, simple pieces. This cut-apart picture becomes a puzzle and can be kept in a box or an envelope to be played with as any puzzle.

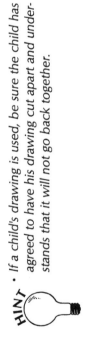

HINT · If a child's drawing is used, be sure the child has agreed to have his drawing cut apart and understands that it will not go back together.

Finger Puppets

Materials

felt pieces, about 3" x 2" (8 cm x 5 cm)

sewing machine

fabric scraps, buttons, sequins, feathers and craft eyes

white glue or hobby glue

felt pens

scissors

Art Process

1. **Adult** cuts two pieces of felt, about three inches long by two inches wide.
2. Place one piece of felt on top of the other and sew a zigzag stitch around the felt, making the top rounded and leaving the bottom open for finger access.
3. Have the artist glue any materials to the base to create an animal, person or character. Use felt pens to add features.
4. Dry the puppet.
5. Make up stories, plays or dances using the finger puppets as the main characters.

Variations

· Cut the fingers off an old glove and make each glove segment a puppet.
· Make puppets from a favorite book and act out the story with the puppets.
· Sing a song with the finger puppets.

HINT

· Some young artists may be able to sew the base together with supervision.
· Measurements can be adjusted for size.

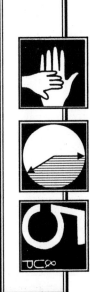

C R A F T

Paper Strip Sculpture

Materials

styrofoam grocery tray for a base
strips of construction paper
tape, glue and stapler
paper punch
scissors

Art Process

1. Attach one end of a paper strip to the grocery tray base using a stapler or tape.
2. Secure another strip to the first one with tape, glue or a stapler.
3. Continue adding strips of paper to the base or to the other strips of paper. Strips can be pleated, folded, connected, cut, paper-punched or fringed with scissors. Let the artists use their imagination!
4. The goal is to create a three-dimensional paper sculpture. Once this has been accomplished and the artist is satisfied with the art, the project is complete.
5. Dry the project completely if glue was used.

Variations

- Add other items to the sculpture such as paper shapes, glitter, confetti, magazine pictures or strips. The artist may also sew and tie pieces of yarn to the sculpture.
- Use other materials to complete this project. Choose items such as matte board or wood for the base. Use other types of paper such as computer paper or wrapping paper to create the sculpture. Join the paper together with stickers or paper-clips.

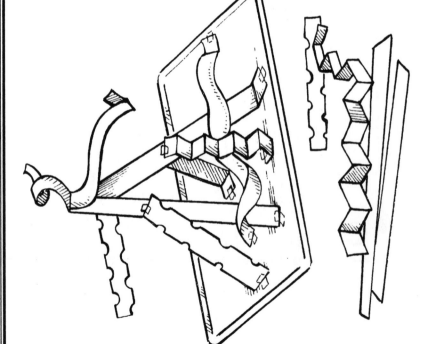

HINT · Paper Strip Sculpture is interesting because of the interaction of paper strips and does not need to "be" anything or look like anything.

CONSTRUCTION

Dark Sugar Chalk

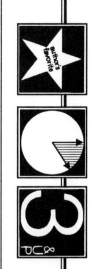

Materials

colored chalk
black paper or matte board
1/3 cup (70 g) sugar dissolved in 1 cup (230 ml) water
cotton balls, optional

Art Process

1. Soak chalk sticks in the cup of sugar water for five to ten minutes. This adds brilliance to the color and helps resist smudging.
2. Draw on the black paper with the sugar chalk. Lines can be bold and bright or light and blurry.
3. Brush chalk marks with cotton balls as an optional art technique.

Variations

- Make a spooky fall drawing. The black background will make the colors seem to glow.
- Use other colors and different textures of paper.
- Paint the paper with a mixture of canned milk and liquid starch. Draw on the wet paper for a sparkling effect.

HINT · Chalk is inherently smudgy, but the sugar-water mixture will help reduce smudging.

Handful Scribble

Materials

handful of crayons all the same length
rubber band
paper
masking tape
music, optional

Art Process

1. Tape a piece of paper to the table to prevent slipping.
2. Bundle a handful of crayons (three or more) with a rubber band. Tap the bundle on the paper to make sure all the crayon points are even.
3. Scribble and color on the paper watching the rainbow effect of many crayons making the same marks.
4. Add music to the scribbling and make marks or strokes that show how the music feels. Remove tape and turn the paper adding more musical scribbles.

Variations

- Use the scribbled paper for a crayon resist by painting over the design with a wash of blue, black or purple paint.
- Use the artwork for wrapping paper.
- Use the scribbled paper as a background for a framed picture or as the background for a finger painting.

HINT · Artists become very energetic when music is added. Using large paper on the floor or wall can accommodate "dancing arms."

D R A W I N G

Sponge Chalk

Materials

large, flat wet sponge
colored chalk
paper

Art Process

1. Draw freely on the wet sponge with chalk.
2. Press the sponge onto paper to transfer a print of the sponge design to the paper.

Variation

• Grind, crush or grate chalk into a dish. Dip pieces of wet sponge into the chalk and dab them on the paper.

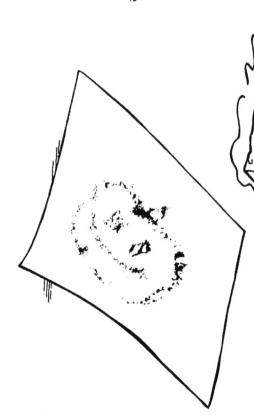

HINT • Chalk breaks often which is perfectly chalk-like. Just use the small pieces until they are too small to hold. Save the tiny pieces to grind or crush into powder for other art projects.

D
R
A
W
I
N
G

Spider Web

Materials

square of plywood, about 3′ (1 m) square
pencils, crayons and felt pens
several nails
hammer
heavy string
chalk
paper
masking tape

Art Process

1. Hammer a nail near the top edge of the plywood square. Be careful not to hammer through the wood and into the floor or table.

2. Tie one end of a two to three foot piece of heavy string to the nail.

3. Place a sheet of paper in the center of the board.

4. Rub chalk back and forth on the string until the string is coated.

5. Hold the loose end of the string with one hand and pull it very tight over the paper. Use the other hand to lift the center of the string, then let go, snapping it against the paper. A puff of chalk will snap against the paper and leave a soft line.

6. Turn the paper. Rub more chalk on the string. Snap it to release another line that crosses the first.

7. Continue turning the paper and snapping chalk lines until the design begins to resemble the framework of a spider web.

8. When ready, move the paper to a table and add the connecting spider web lines with chalk, pencil, felt pen or crayon. Add a spider too, if desired.

HINT

- White chalk on black paper is effective but various colors on white or black paper are pretty too.

- When the chalk sticks are rubbed back and forth, the string scores the chalk and the stick breaks easily. Use these small pieces to continue rubbing the string. When pieces are too small to handle, save them for other art activities where chalk is crushed or grated.

- Keep in mind some artists will create a design instead of a spider web.

Buttermilk Chalk Screen

Materials
wire mesh screen (stapled to back of old picture frame)
colored chalk
buttermilk in cup
paintbrush
paper
covered work area

Art Process
1. Place a sheet of paper on the work area.
2. Paint the paper with buttermilk.
3. Place the picture frame with screen on the paper. The wire mesh should be on the back of the frame and up off the paper.
4. Rub colored chalk back and forth over the screen so that powdered bits of chalk fall into the buttermilk on the paper beneath.
5. Try different colors of chalk and different areas of the screen.
6. Lift the frame and screen and watch the effect of the chalk absorbing the buttermilk on the paper as a sparkled result occurs.
7. Dry the chalk art completely.

Variations
• This project can be repeated with paint spattered through the screen from a nail brush or toothbrush.
• Paint the paper with a combination of liquid starch and canned milk instead of buttermilk for a similar effect.
• Place paper shapes or stencils on the paper before rubbing the chalk through the screen. After chalking, remove the stencils and see the design left on the paper.

HINT
• Be sure the screen is securely stapled to the back of the frame. Reinforce with duct tape if necessary. Young artists tend to press hard on the screen and it can tear away from the frame if not secure.
• If you don't have buttermilk, add a 1/2 t of vinegar to regular milk and let it sit for five minutes. Do not drink.

DRAWING

4

PC8

Mystery Paint

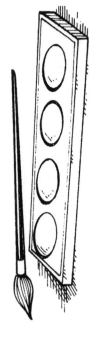

Materials

4 tablespoons baking soda
4 tablespoons water
cup to mix soda and water
cotton swabs
sheet of white paper
watercolor paint
paintbrush

Art Process

1. Dissolve the baking soda and water in a cup.
2. Dip the cotton swab in the mixture and paint an invisible picture on the white paper.
3. Dry the artwork completely.
4. Brush the watercolor paint over the paper to reveal the mystery picture.

Variations

- Create a secret picture for a friend to reveal with watercolor paint.
- Create a secret message for a friend
- Add crayon to the mystery painting and then brush with water color paint for a mystery wax resist.

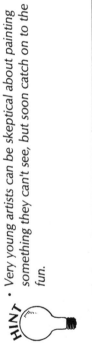

HINT · Very young artists can be skeptical about painting something they can't see, but soon catch on to the fun.

PAINTING

Fingerprints

Materials

choose one of the following for the color:

- food coloring (dip fingers in liquid placed in a jar lid)
- felt pens (color fingertips)
- ink pads (press fingertips onto pad)
- tempera paints (press fingertips on pads of damp paper towels and paint)

paper

fine tip felt pens for adding features

soapy water in bucket and towel for clean up

Art Process

1. First choose one of the coloring methods.
2. Color a favorite finger or thumb with the chosen color.
3. Press the colored finger onto the paper. The artist may press several times before re-coloring.
4. Dry the artwork.
5. Add details to the fingerprints with fine felt tip markers such as features, hats, cars or feet.

Variation

- Draw a picture with a crayon and then add fingerprints to enhance the drawing. Some examples include: fingerprint blossoms in a crayon tree or flower pot, fingerprint hair on a funny face or fingerprint bugs on a crayon branch.

HINT

- Some artists enjoy messy hands and fingers; other artists find the mess almost unbearable. Some of the aversion is due to a developmentally recognized correlation between messy hands and potty training. The aversion usually passes and artists become comfortable with messy hands and fingers again as they get older.

PAINTING

Tilt Prints

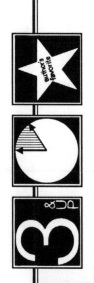

Materials
items to use for printing such as small balls, nuts and bolts, marbles, pieces of small toys or other small rolling items
several colors of tempera paint in cups with spoons
shallow baking pan
paper to fit pan
bowl of soapy water and towels

Art Process
1. Place the paper in the baking pan.
2. Select some rolling items such as nuts and bolts or marbles.
3. With a spoon drop puddles of paint on the paper.
4. Drop the rolling items into the pan and tilt the pan around, rolling them through the paint and making designs on the paper.
5. Dry the completed artwork.
6. To wash up, drop painted items into the bowl of soapy water and wash. Wash hands too. Dry the items and hands.

Variations
• Use a round cake pan with a paper plate in it.
• Put a puddle of paint on an incline board covered with paper and roll the same items through the paint down the board.
• Roll hard-boiled eggs through paint puddles in a plastic dish pan to decorate the eggs.

HINT
• Experiment with different items to roll. Some items make amazing prints that surprise everyone.
• Items used for tilt prints may not come completely clean.

PAINTING

Chalk Paint

Materials

cheese grater
colored chalk
wax paper square
muffin tin
cotton swabs
water in small dishes
paper

Art Process

1. **Adult** helps the artist grate colored chalk onto a square of wax paper. Shake the chalk gratings into a muffin cup.
2. Dip a cotton swab into water and then into the powdered, grated chalk and paint on the paper freely.
3. Dry the project completely.

Variations

• Put powdered tempera paint in separate muffin cups. Paint by dipping cotton swabs in the water and then into the powdered paint.
• Experiment with other drawing or painting tools such as a paint-brush, feather or finger.
• Work on paper that has been pre-moistened with water, butter-milk or a mixture of liquid starch and canned milk.

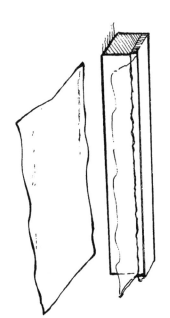

HINT

• For a fine powdered chalk, crush the chalk with a hammer or rock instead of using a cheese grater.
• Art chalk works better than the dustless chalkboard variety of chalk.

PAINTING

Shoe Polish Leaves

Materials

supple autumn leaves
shoe polish in bottle with applicator (variety of colors)
variety of papers
covered work surface
extra sheets of newsprint
bucket of soapy water
nail brush
towel

Art Process

1. Collect fresh autumn leaves in a variety of shapes and sizes.
2. Place a leaf on a piece of newsprint, face side down.
3. Dab shoe polish over the back surface of the leaf.
4. Select a piece of paper and lay it gently on the shoe polished leaf. Press and pat the paper gently over the leaf.
5. Peel the paper and leaf apart revealing a shoe polish leaf print on the paper.
6. Select another leaf, change polish colors or make a print on a new sheet of newsprint.

Variations

- Place a leaf on a sheet of paper. Dab shoe polish around the edges of the leaf, brushing out from the edges onto the paper. Remove the leaf and a stencil design will be left.
- Experiment with patterns and designs, types of paper and colors of shoe polish.

HINT
- *Shoe polish stains hands and fingernails. Have a soapy bucket of water close by with nail brush and towel for clean up.*
- *Shoe polish leaf prints show the veins and features of leaves in detail.*

PAINTING

Jacko-Cheese

Materials
2 cups (400 g) grated cheddar cheese
1/4 cup (50 g) flour
2 tablespoons mayonnaise
bowl
clean work surface
square of wax paper
clean hands
plastic knife, toothpick and other kitchen tools

Art Process
1. With adult help, mix the cheese, flour and mayonnaise in a bowl with clean hands. Squeeze and blend the ingredients until the consistency of dough. Add more flour if the dough is too sticky and more cheese or mayonnaise if the dough is too stiff or dry.
2. Place a ball of cheese dough on a square of wax paper on a clean work surface.
3. Mold, pat and sculpt the cheese dough into a flattened oval or circle resembling a pumpkin.
4. With a plastic knife or other kitchen tool, dig or cut away holes for the pumpkin's face.
5. Leave the jacko-face on the wax paper square and save in the refrigerator to eat later.
6. Make as many cheese sculptures or faces as desired.

Variation
· Use white cheese and make little cheese ghosts with faces.

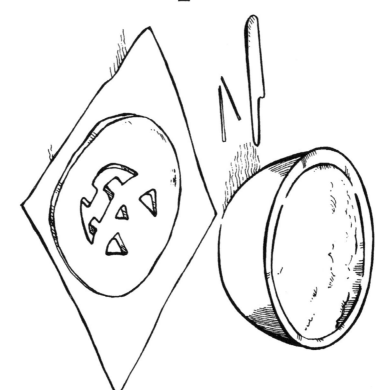

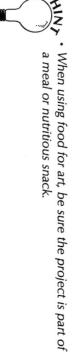

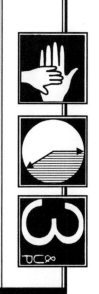

HINT · When using food for art, be sure the project is part of a meal or nutritious snack.

D
O
U
G
H

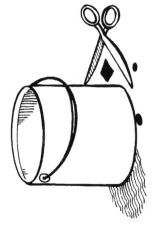

Pumpkin Face Mystery

Materials
scrap black paper
box or bucket
orange paper
glue or tape
scissors

Art Process
1. With adult help, cut black paper into strange or realistic shapes to suggest a mouth, eyes, nose or other facial feature. Shapes can be very large or very small.
2. Place these black scrap features into a box or bucket.
3. With adult help, cut orange paper into circles and ovals of all sizes ranging from very large to very small.
4. Place a few orange circles or ovals on the floor.
5. Reach into the box and pull out a black scrap. Place the scrap on the circle or oval to begin building a face for a pumpkin. Features can be silly, realistic, scary or any style desired. The fun of this project is the mystery of how the pumpkin face will turn out since it is created by drawing the features randomly from a box.
6. Make several different pumpkin faces. Play by changing the features around to see what different expressions and personalities can be created.
7. If desired, tape or glue the features in place and hang the completed pumpkin faces in a window, on a wall or as a doorway decoration.

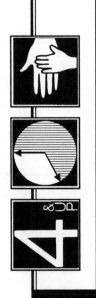

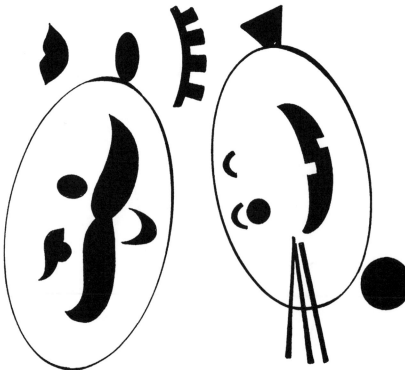

HINT • Some artists will choose to create random designs instead of pumpkin faces. Allow for creativity and imagination.

COLLAGE

Impress Wall Pot

Materials
salt, flour and water to make baker's clay (see recipe below)
measuring cup
rolling pin
other kitchen tools such as a spatula or knife
items to press into clay such as toys, buttons, fork,
    nuts, bolt or a pencil
cookie sheet
oven preheated to 300 degrees
yarn
collection of dried weeds and grasses from outside

Art Process
1. Make the baker's clay by hand mixing one cup salt, four cups flour and one and one-half cups water in a bowl. Knead the mixture for five minutes until soft and pliable.
2. Place two balls of clay on the table and roll each one out flat. Place one piece on a cookie sheet.
3. Decorate the clay by pressing toys or other items into it.
4. Carefully lift the decorated piece and lay it on top of the plain piece. Lift the top edge of the top piece of clay to create an envelope-like opening. Press the rest of the edges together with a fork or pinch with the fingers. Poke two little holes in the top of the clay envelope for hanging with yarn later.
5. Bake the completed pots in a 300 degree oven for about an hour or two or until nicely browned and hard all the way through.
6. **Adult** removes the pots from the oven.

7. When cool, stick bits of weeds, dried flowers or grasses into the opening of the "envelope."
8. Add a yarn piece through the holes in the top of the design and hang the finished pot on the wall as a decoration.

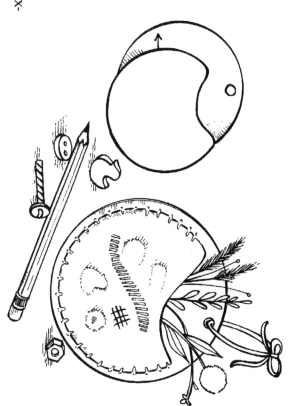

HINT · Experiment and explore with various doughs and clays before attempting to make this project. Many artists need to know how each dough acts before making a craft or sculpture.

Weaving Board

Materials

flat scrap of wood for weaving board (piece of a one by ten)

finishing nails (no head)

hammer

heavy string

yarn

other weaving materials such as strips of fabric, ribbon, dry grass, sewing trim, crepe paper or raffia

scissors

Art Process

1. **Adult** helps hammer nails into two edges of a flat board from one quarter inch to one inch apart. Help the artist hammer nails so they are in tight and firm but not poking through the other side of the wood.

2. Help the artist wrap heavy string back and forth from one end of the board to the other. Start with the first nail and end with the last nail. Tie the string securely. The heavy string is called the warp.

3. With colorful yarn, ribbon, strips of fabric or other long material (called the woof), push the woof string under and over the heavy warp strings. There is no need to weave in a specific style.

4. Change colors and materials, if desired, and continue weaving in any way, form or pattern. Tuck in loose ends or tie the end of one loose end to the beginning of the next.

5. Weave until the warp strings are completely full.

6. Remove the warp from the nails when complete or leave the artwork on the weaving board for display.

STEP 1

STEP 2

HINT
- Allow for exploration with many weaving materials and activities. Then demonstrate the over-under technique and the over-two-under-one pattern. Because the artist is experienced, the demonstrations will make more sense.

CRAFT

Stocking Mask

Materials

nylon stocking or panty hose
wire coat hanger
ribbon or rubber band
fabric scraps, buttons, yarn, paper clips, beads, old jewelry or
   earrings or rug scraps to make the face
glue or needle and thread

Art Process

1. **Adult** helps round out a wire coat hanger with the hook at the
   base, to resemble the shape of a hand mirror.
2. Cut the stocking as shown in the illustration. Two masks can be
   made from each leg of a stocking.
3. Pull the section of stocking with the foot attached over the coat
   hanger and secure with a ribbon or rubber band at the hooked
   end of the hanger. If the thigh section of the stocking is used,
   both the top and the base must be tied around the hanger.
4. Make a face on the stretched stocking with scraps, buttons, yarn
   or other decorative items. Glue or hand stitch the pieces on the
   stocking mask.
5. When dry, hold the stocking mask up to the face and speak or
   act while hiding behind it.

Variation

· If a wire hanger is not available, an adult can cut an oval of
   heavy cardboard into a mask shape and cut out the middle for
   the stocking face. This material may not be as strong as the wire
   hanger so the stocking may need to be cut into a single layer,
   stretched and stapled or taped to the cardboard.

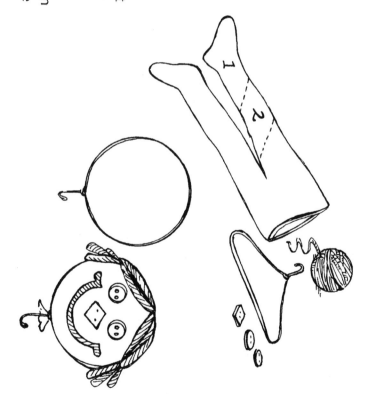

HINT

· Be aware that very young children can be frightened
   of masks because they have not yet learned to
   separate fantasy and reality.

· Masks can make a shy child daring, a gentle child
   rough, a bold child quiet or a rough child gentle
   thereby revealing any number of secrets and
   surprises.

C
R
A
F
T

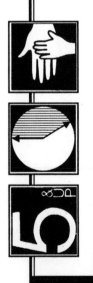

Ghost Tree

Materials

tree branch
coffee can filled with sand
colored paper
heavy paper towels
scissors

glue
cotton balls, optional
black felt pen
thread
tape

Art Process

1. Stick the end of a branch in a coffee can. Add sand around the branch so the Ghost Tree won't tip over. Cover the can with colored paper. Set this aside.
2. Draw a ghostly shape with glue on a heavy paper towel.
3. Press another paper towel to the first. You may choose to leave the bottom of the shape open to stuff and glue later. Dry the ghost.
4. Draw a face on the ghostly shape with the black pen.
5. Cut out the ghostly shape. If an opening was left at the bottom of the ghost, stuff the shape with cotton balls. Glue the end closed.
6. Tape or stitch a piece of thread to the ghost's head and hang the ghost from the tree branch.
7. Make more ghosts to hang from the branch until the sculpture is complete.

Variations

• Instead of ghosts make stuffed snowflakes, bears, hearts or geometric shapes. Experiment with papers of all types.
• Trace a hand on a doubled paper towel and make a ghost mitten or ghost puppet.

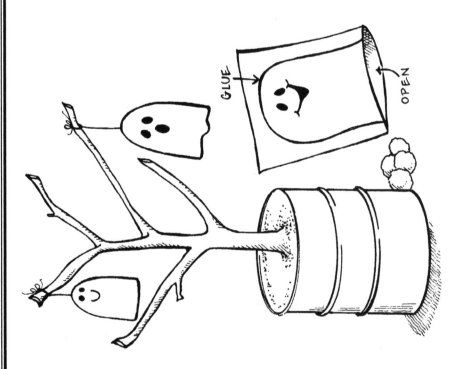

GLUE

OPEN

HINT • Paper can be sewn on a sewing machine instead of using glue. Use a long stitch or a zigzag stitch.

CRAFT

Harvest Art

Materials

leftover harvest foods in the field, orchard or garden such as corn husks, leaves, twigs, berries or nuts

toothpicks, wooden matches, bamboo skewers, straight pins or string

bits of paper, play clay, feathers or dried flowers

permanent felt pens

Art Process

1. Go for a walk in a field, orchard or garden and collect leftover harvest foods or other outdoor materials.
2. Create corn husk royalty, corn folks, nut puppets, stick marionettes, feather birds, leaf masks or any other imaginative mobiles or designs.
3. Use string, skewers, toothpicks or other ideas to assemble the harvest art.
4. Add berries for eyes, bits of paper for capes and hats and pen marks for features. There really is no right or wrong way to create harvest art. The fun is being outside on a crisp day hunting for treasures from the earth to make things.
5. Take a few of the collected vegetables or fruits home to cook.
6. Bring the art home to enjoy or leave for critters to discover and eat.

Variation

- Build little houses for the creatures from ferns, moss, sticks and holes dug into the earth. Add roads, worlds and more worlds.

HINT

- Most of the Harvest Art creations will not hold together well for robust play. Enjoy creating and playing on the day the art is made and prepare to bid them farewell fairly soon thereafter.

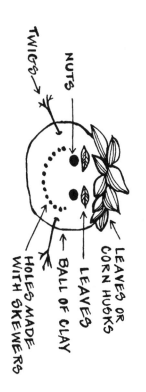

TWIGS →

NUTS

LEAVES OR CORN HUSKS

LEAVES

BALL OF CLAY

HOLES MADE WITH SKEWERS

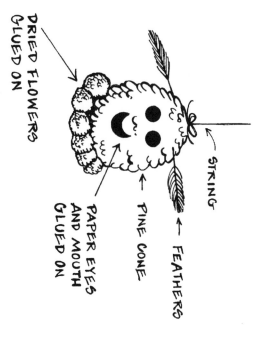

DRIED FLOWERS GLUED ON

STRING

PINE CONE

FEATHERS

PAPER EYES AND MOUTH GLUED ON

C R A F T

Big Spooky House

Materials

large cardboard panel
knife and scissors
tempera paint and paintbrushes
paper
crayons
masking tape

Art Process

1. **Adult** helps cut the cardboard panel to look like a roof shape at the top. Under the direction of the artist, cut as many doors and windows as desired. Leave one side of the openings "hinged" so doors and windows will open and shut or cut a "capital I" shape so the openings open from the center and fold back.

2. Place the panel flat on the floor and paint the house to have boards, bricks, shutters, shingles and other details. Dry completely.

3. Make spooky drawings on paper large enough to fit over the window and door openings. Draw ghosts, bats, pumpkins, trick-or-treaters and other Halloween images.

4. Tape the pictures over the openings from the back so the tape doesn't show.

5. Lean the spooky house panel up against a wall or door where it can be secured to stand on its own with tape or some other method.

6. Enjoy opening and closing the spooky doors and windows.

Variation

- Instead of a spooky Halloween theme, design a house, tree or vehicle with other types of characters inside. Some suggestions include forest creatures, storybook characters or aliens from another planet.

HINT • Be prepared for some screams of delight
• Make smaller spooky houses with construction paper or smaller pieces of cardboard.

Peeky Panel

Materials
cardboard panel, about child-sized
   (cut from refrigerator or appliance box)
knife and scissors
white chalk
tempera paints

large, flat paintbrushes
small, fine paintbrushes
large floor space for working

Art Process
1. **Adult** helps trim the cardboard to chin-height of the artist. Next cut a half circle into the top edge of the cardboard. Hand holes will be added later.
2. Place the cardboard flat on the floor. Using chalk, have the artist sketch a comical or realistic human form. Chalk can be rubbed off to change lines.
3. When the drawing is complete, an **adult** can cut the two circles for the hands or arms.
4. Next, place the cardboard flat again and paint the sketched body. Paint large areas first with a large flat brush. Let the paint dry. Use a small brush to paint the smaller more refined areas.
5. Add background in addition to details such as an umbrella in the hand or a dog on a leash. Dry the panel completely.
6. When dry, stand behind the panel, insert hands or arms through the two holes and rest the chin in the oval. Do this in front of a mirror or have a friend take a picture.

Variation
• With a small piece of cardboard, cut out a face shape. Design this panel with hair, a hat, ears, jewelry or other features. The artist may use this like a mask.

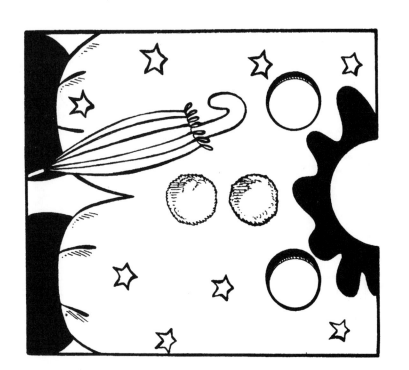

HINT • Young artists enjoy the comical possibilities of this art form which also helps expand their awareness of the human form.

Crayon Hands

Materials

crayons

pencils

colored paper and paper scraps

scissors

glue, tape, a stapler or brads

Art Process

1. Use a crayon or pencil to trace the artist's hands on a piece of paper. Some artists prefer to trace their own hands without help.

2. Cut out the hand shapes. Trace and cut as many hand shapes as necessary for the chosen project. The design idea may be planned before the project is begun or evolve as the hands are traced.

3. Look over the hand shapes and try to think of something that could be made with the cutouts. Some suggestions are a turkey, ghost, reindeer antlers, cat, chick, duck, bunny, angel wings, tulips, a butterfly, or random hand designs.

4. Glue the hand shapes to paper and add other paper scraps or drawings to complete the design. Simply gluing hand shapes in an interesting, design is enjoyable too.

5. Dry the completed project.

Variations

· Use tracing and cutouts of bare feet for art ideas.

· Use brads for moving parts of the design.

HINT · Once young artists get the idea of seeing shapes in common objects, such as hands used for deer antlers, they will discover many shapes in all parts of their visual world.

DRAWING

Candle Crayons

Materials

candles (all shapes, sizes and colors)
white paper
watercolor paints and paintbrush
cup of water
crayons, optional
covered work surface

Art Process

1. Place a sheet of paper on the covered work surface.
2. Draw with candles of any size, shape and color. Press hard for visible marks from many candles.
3. For an optional idea, draw and color with crayon on the candle drawing.
4. To see the candle drawing, paint over the drawing with water-color paint. This is called a wax resist.
5. Dry the project completely. If drawing is very wrinkled or curled, iron the back of the paper with a warm iron to flatten.

Variations

- Write secret messages with candles or draw pictures of a cele-bration on white butcher paper covering a party table. Give each party guest a cup of colored water and a paintbrush to uncover the secrets on the table.
- A wash of thinned tempera paint or ink works as well as the watercolor paints.
- A dramatic wax resist can be achieved by coloring very hard and brightly on paper with crayons and painting over the drawing with black or dark blue tempera paint.

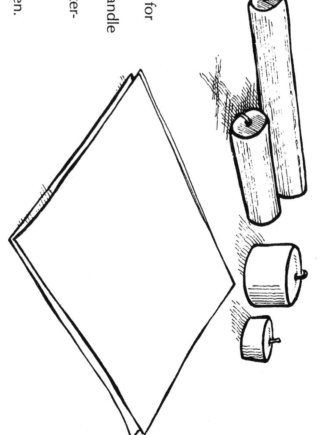

HINT
- Rinse brush between colors in the plain water. Change water often for truest colors.
- Press hard with candles for a drawing that works with the watercolor paints.

D
R
A
W
I
N
G

Fuzzy Glue Drawing

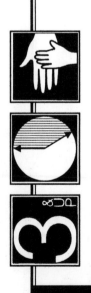

Materials

scissors

yarn in contrasting colors to the background

plastic bag or plastic container with lid for yarn snips

white glue in a dish (to color white glue, mix with food coloring or tempera paint)

paintbrush for glue

paper plate or matte board for the base

covered work surface

Art Process

1. Wind some yarn about fifteen times around your fingers. Cut through the end of the loops.

2. Snip small pieces of the yarn one-half inch or smaller into the plastic bag or container. (Cut different lengths or different colors if desired.)

3. Have the artist paint glue over a small area of the base.

4. The artist can choose a color of yarn and pat it down into the glued area.

5. Paint more glue in a different area and pat more yarn into that glue. Continue making glue and yarn designs or continue until the entire base is full.

Variation

• Cut different colors of yarn and draw a picture with a glue bottle to create fuzzy yarn pictures. Always work on small areas rather than large areas so glue won't dry out before the yarn has been attached.

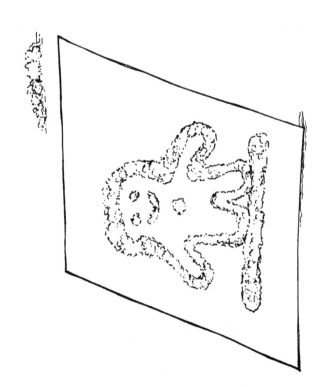

HINT • The one trick to a successful project is to spread the glue onto the base and press the yarn into the glue. Do not dip the yarn into the glue in the dish.

• Adults can help with hand-wiping and yarn-snipping but the artists should draw and cover the glue pictures.

DRAWING

Transparent Crayon

Materials
white paper
crayons
cooking oil
cotton balls
newspaper to cover table

Art Process
1. Place white paper on the newspaper.
2. Draw freely with crayon on the white paper, pressing hard.
3. Rub a small amount of cooking oil over the back of the white paper using a cotton ball.
4. Dry the oil and crayon design on fresh newspaper.

Variations
- Use baby oil or mineral oil in place of cooking oil.
- Use a paintbrush to spread the oil instead of cotton balls.
- Experiment with different types of paper.

HINT
- Have a bucket of soapy warm water handy to wash oily hands.
- Some artists may not like the feeling or results of oil. Remember this is normal for young children.

DRAWING

Dot Dots

Materials

any drawing or coloring tools such as crayons, felt pens, paints and brushes, chalk, oil pastels or colored pencils
paper

Art Process

1. Create an entire drawing or design using only dots of color.
2. Change colors as desired.
3. Combine different art media such as using crayon dots for part of the design and paint dots for the background.

Variations

• Use contrasting colors such as green dots on red paper or yellow dots on purple paper.
• Pointillism is a technique of making paintings using nothing but dots to create a larger picture. This technique can easily be explored by young artists.

HINT
• Look through a magnifying glass at the Sunday comics, coloring books in color or comic books and see how dots make up the entire picture. Young artists can usually understand the approach of Dot Dots drawing after looking through the magnifying glass or looking at the work of pointillism artists such as Seurat.

DRAWING

Corncob Print

Materials

dried corncobs without kernels
tempera paint on cookie sheet
corn holders or nails
large paper
covered work area

Art Process

1. Save corncobs after corn has been eaten and dry them on a shelf.
2. Pour puddles of paint on a cookie sheet or tray.
3. Push corn holders into the ends of the corn cob to use as handles while painting. If holders are not available, an **adult** can push nails into each end of the cob. If this doesn't work, just hold the ends of the cob with fingers.
4. Roll the corn cob through the paint on the cookie sheet like a paint roller.
5. Roll the paint covered cob across the large sheet of paper. Roll one long line or use back and forth movements. Make designs or any other shapes.
6. Dry the artwork.

Variation

· Use the corn cob print for gift wrap or backgrounds for other projects.

HINT

· Sometimes this project works best on the floor so active artists can really roll the corn.
· Corn cobs can be rinsed in water, dried and used again.

PAINTING

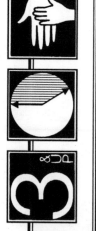

Negative Space

Materials
large newsprint
scissors
paint easel
paints and brushes
drying rack

Art Process
1. With adult help cut a hole or shape out of the newsprint to be used for easel painting.
2. Attach the newsprint to the easel.
3. Paint on the paper using the negative space as part of the painting.
4. Remove the artwork from the easel and place on a drying rack.

Variations
- Cut paper into shapes for painting on the easel.
- Glue a colored shape on the newsprint to incorporate in the painting.
- Use all of the negative space or shape ideas above with crayons or pens on paper.

HINT · *Many artists are uncomfortable with a hole in the middle of their papers. Encourage them to enjoy the paper with the negative space.*

PAINTING

Finger Paint Mono-Stencil

Materials
scrap construction paper
scissors
loop of masking tape
finger paint (tempera paint and liquid starch)
cookie sheet or table top
big paper
newspaper for drying paintings
bucket of soapy water and towel for clean up

Art Process
1. Cut a shape out of construction paper such as a circle, a leaf, any design or shape.
2. Tape the shape to the center of a sheet of paper with a loop of masking tape on the back of the shape. Set the paper aside.
3. Pour a puddle of liquid starch in the middle of the cookie sheet. Place a spoonful of liquid tempera paint or powdered tempera paint in the starch puddle.
4. Mix the starch and paint with the hands and continue finger painting on the cookie sheet. (If the paint is "resisting" add a few drops of liquid detergent to the finger paint.)
5. When the finger painting on the cookie sheet is complete, help the artist place the paper with the shape (shape side down) over the cookie sheet. Gently press and pat the paper to the finger painting design for a mono-print.
6. Peel the paper from the cookie sheet and place it on some newspaper to dry.
7. Gently peel or pull the paper shape from the painting; the unpainted shape will be surrounded by finger painting.

HINT
· Have damp rags handy for the artist to wipe fingers and hands.
· The drying area should be next to the printing area.

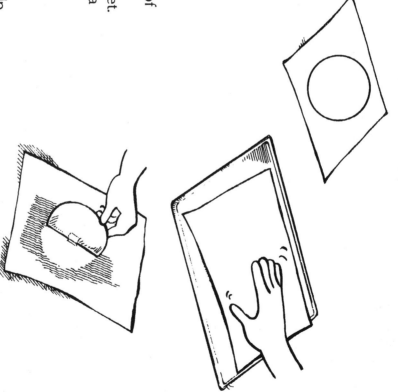

PAINTING

Twist and Shout

Materials
squeeze bottles filled with tempera paints
heavy paper
floor covered with newsprint
large scrap of laminate from a counter top for paint surface
sponges and soapy water for clean up

Art Process
1. Squeeze three to four big drops of paint directly on the scrap of counter top laminate on the floor.
2. Place a piece of heavy paper on the drops of paint.
3. Twist the paper with the heel of the palm about half a turn.
4. Lift and see the design.
5. Continue to experiment with colors and types of twisting to create new designs.
6. Sponge off the laminate with soapy water to make way for new creations or a change of artists.

Variations
- Make twisting designs with bare feet with or without paper.
- Use a paper plate or other types of paper for the twisting design.
- Use a table instead of the laminate from a counter top.
- Work on a cookie sheet instead of a table or laminate.

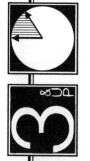

HINT
- An adult should keep the laminate clean between artists or when a new creation is started. For this reason, this activity would work well outdoors where a bucket or hose could easily do the job.

PAINTING

Palette Paint

Materials
frozen dinner tray
tempera paints
paintbrush
jar of water and rag
paint easel
paper

Art Process
1. Place blobs of paint on a frozen dinner tray.
2. Have the artist stand at an easel holding the tray in one hand like a palette. Using one brush, mix shades and tints of paint on the palette to apply to the paper.
3. Rinse the brush in the water often. Use the rag to dry the paintbrush as necessary.

Variations
- Use a pie plate or styrofoam lid instead of a frozen dinner plate for the palette. Use a real paint palette.
- Provide a palette knife (any plastic knife or craft stick will do) to experience dabbing and spreading paint on the easel.
- Some artists can experiment with acrylic paints.

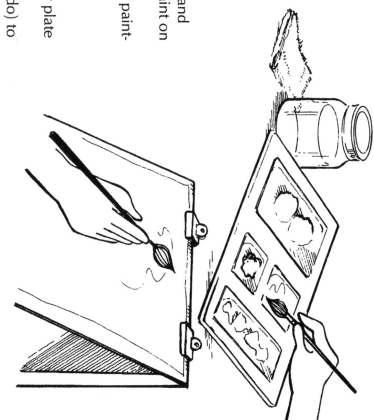

HINT
- Palette painting is an advanced step to be explored after a child has had some experience mixing paints in other art experiences. Young artists like to pretend they are famous adult artists standing at the easel and painting the way famous artists do. Provide a beret to add a dress-up and pretend element to the activity.

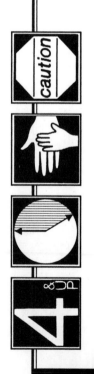

String Thing

Materials

granulated starch   bowl
water   colorful yarn or embroidery floss,
pan   about 1 yard (1 m) long
stove   a strong balloon
spoon   table covered with newspaper

Art Process

1. **Adult** makes the extra strong liquid starch as follows: dissolve one tablespoon of granulated starch in the amount of water stated on the starch package. Follow the rest of the instructions on the package. Place in a bowl and cool.
2. Blow up a balloon. Tie a double knot at the end.
3. Dip a string or yarn in the starch mixture. Make sure it is completely covered with starch but not too heavy to drape around the balloon.
4. Wrap the string around the balloon being sure to plaster down the ends of the string.
5. When the balloon is well covered with string (but not completely covered), dry the balloon overnight.
6. When the string is thoroughly dry, pop the balloon and remove it.
7. Use a piece of thread to hang the String Thing from the ceiling, a branch or from some other framework.

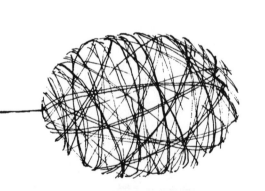

HINT
- *The tendency to over-wrap the balloon is common. If too much string is used, it will just slip off the balloon in a pile on the table. Begin again and use less string.*
- *Gently squeeze some of the starch out of the yarn between two fingers and the yarn will be sticky but not too heavy.*

S
C
U
L
P
T
U
R
E

Stomped Foil Sculpture

Materials

aluminum foil, new or recycled
masking tape
matte board in black or other color

Art Process

1. Take a piece of foil and squeeze or bundle the piece into a ball or other shape.
2. Place the foil shape on the floor.
3. Stomp on it until it is completely flat.
4. Make small loops of masking tape and place them on the back of the flattened foil.
5. Press the flattened foil on the matte board until it sticks. Add more tape if necessary.

Variations

- Color the matte board with chalk or paint for a colorful background for the stomped sculpture.
- Stomped Foil Sculpture can be suspended from the ceiling on black thread.

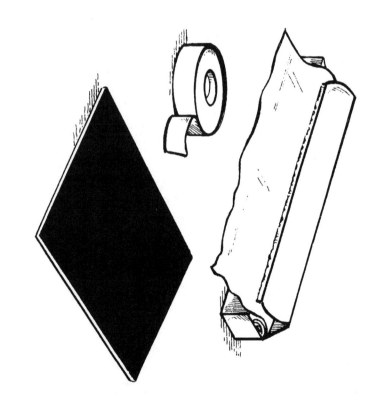

HINT · Stomped sculptures create interesting shapes and are an exhilarating art experiences at any age.

S
C
U
L
P
T
U
R
E

Painted Foil Sculpture

Materials

aluminum foil, recycled or new
matte board or cardboard
glue paint—mix tacky glue with tempera paint and a few drops of
liquid detergent
glue gun, optional (to be used by an adult)
paintbrush

Art Process

1. Form one piece of foil into a shape or sculpture.
2. Mount the sculpture on matte board with tacky glue or glue paint. Allow plenty of time for the glue to dry. A quicker method is to have an adult use a glue gun and stick the foil shape to the matte board. Observe safety.
3. Paint the sculpture with glue paint. This allows the silver to shine through.
4. Dry the sculpture completely.

Variations

- Mix food coloring into the glue for a more transparent glue paint.
- Add more tempera to the glue paint for an opaque glue paint.
- Combine wood scraps or other collage and sculpture materials to the foil sculpture.

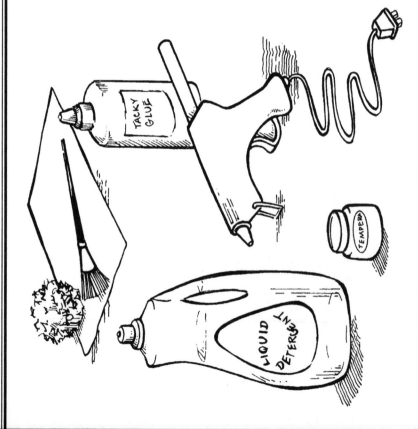

HINT
- *Aluminum foil is a wonderful art medium and is inexpensive and convenient. Allow some experimentation and exploration for the artist. Recycle or reuse first attempts.*
- *Detailed features, extensions or body parts are hard to accomplish with foil. Try to make the sculpture from one piece of foil.*

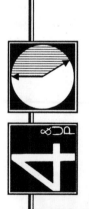

SCULPTURE

Tray Punch and Sew

caution

3 & up

C
R
A
F
T

Materials

styrofoam grocery tray
tool for poking holes, such as pencil or scissors point
pad of newspapers
variety of pre-cut colored yarns, about 2 feet long
masking tape

Art Process

1. Place the styrofoam grocery tray on the pad of newspapers.
2. With **adult** help, poke holes, but not too many, with a pointed tool such as a pencil. (The artist may wish to choose a number, such as ten, and poke only that many holes.)
3. Poke the holes in a random design or poke holes that suggest a picture or shape. More holes can always be poked later or at any time during the project.
4. Wrap masking tape around the end of a piece of yarn to resemble a needle and push through a hole in the tray.
5. Pull the yarn all the way to the end of the yarn. Tape the end of the yarn to the back of the meat tray.
6. Continue sewing in and out of the holes to make a design. Change colors of yarn at any time.
7. When the design is complete, tape the last end of yarn to the back of the meat tray.

Variations

• Sew with yarn threaded on a large plastic needle.
• Do not pre-poke holes in the styrofoam tray. Sew on the grocery tray with yarn threaded on a plastic needle and poke holes as in embroidery.

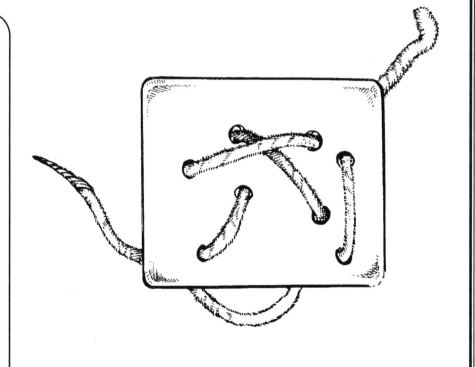

HINT • Young artists need help threading a needle, taping the end of the yarn for a needle and untangling knots and loops that sometimes form.

Masterpiece Collection

Materials

children's artwork
glue and tape
scrap book with blank pages
felt pen

Art Process

1. To save favorite artwork in a scrap book, choose a piece of art and glue or tape it into the scrap book. The book can be organized in specific sections or randomly as the year progresses.
2. An adult may write down the artist's comments about specific artwork placed in the scrap book. Do not write on the artwork. Some questions to ask the artists include: "What did you like about this artwork?," "Tell me about your masterpiece" or "Tell me about the colors you chose."
3. Continue to save flat artwork in the scrap book until it is full.

Variations

- Some artists prefer a scrap book where they create directly on each scrapbook page.
- Make a homemade scrap book. Stack large sheets of paper together. Punch holes on one side of the paper. Punch holes in a cardboard cover. String the scrap book together with yarn and begin saving artwork or photographs in this homemade scrap book.

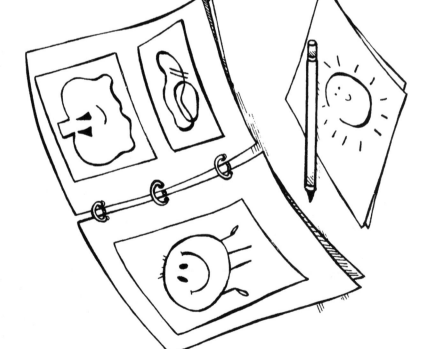

HINT · The artist should chose what to save for the collection.

Cuff Finger Puppets

Materials
old pair of pants with deep cuffs or hem
sewing machine
scissors
materials for decorating the puppets including sewing scraps, yarn,
buttons, plastic eyes or felt
tacky glue or needle and thread

Art Process
1. Turn an old pair of pants with deep cuffs inside out. Cut straight
across the hem.
2. With adult help sew two "U" shapes on each cuff so that the
hem of the cuff will be the bottom of each finger puppet. Cut
one-third inch from the edge of the sewn line. Turn the cuff
right-side out or leave as is.
3. Decorate the cuff puppets with any variety of sewing or craft
items using glue or a needle and thread. Puppets can be
animals, people, characters from a book or story or strange little
shapes with no real adult understanding.
4. Make up plays, songs or simply enjoy the puppets.

Variation
• Decorate a box for storing a growing collection of cuff puppets.
Develop a group of puppets that can be stored together such as
the three cuff bears and one golden haired cuff girl.

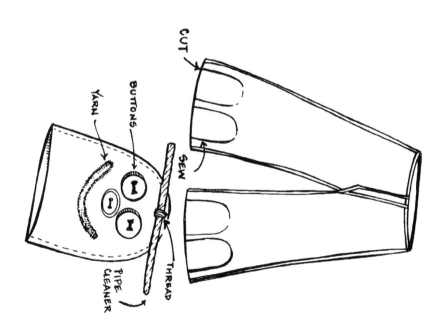

HINT • Each pair of pants makes approximately four cuff
puppets.

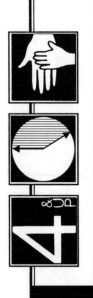

C
R
A
F
T

Easy Store Puppet Stage

Materials

one spring-tension curtain rod to fit a doorway
old sheet
fabric pens
glue paints (tacky glue and tempera paint mixed together)
dishes for paints
paintbrushes
sewing machine, optional

Art Process

1. Spread a spring-tension curtain rod in a doorway at a height suitable for young puppeteers.
2. With fabric pens or glue paint, decorate an old sheet for the puppet curtain. Dry the curtain completely.
3. Drape the sheet over the rod and produce a puppet show by crouching behind the curtain.
4. As an optional idea, sew a simple casing at the top of a decorated sheet cut to fit the doorway and rod. Push the curtain rod through the casing and place it in the doorway.
5. To store the puppet stage, roll the curtain up around the rod and put it in any corner or spare closet space.

Variation

• Make a glamorous curtain by adding glitter to the wet glue paint.

HINT · Remember that sometimes puppeteers need help winding up a long production with a gentle hint that the show will end in a few more minutes.

Circle Weave

Materials

matte board or cardboard cut into circles, any size

scissors

yarns, many colors cut about 2 feet (70 cm) long

masking tape

Art Process

1. With adult help cut cardboard or matte board into circles of any size. About five inches across is a manageable size for young hands.

2. Help the artist cut about five or six slits around the edge of each circle with scissors.

3. Weave the circle shape by winding yarn around and around the circle taking the yarn through one of the slits with each pass. Experiment with crisscross designs.

4. Tape or tie the end of the yarn on the back of the circle. Bend in the edges between the slits, if desired.

Variations

- Cut other shapes from matte board or cardboard such as a tree, square or heart.
- Use embroidery floss in place of yarn.

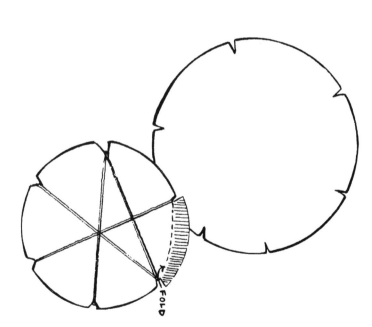

FOLD

HINT

- For an easy yarn dispenser, place a ball of yarn in a margarine cup. Cut a hole in the lid of the cup. Pull the yarn end through the hole and then snap on the lid. The yarn will unwind without tangling.

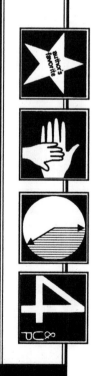

Scrimshaw Pendant

Materials

1/3 cup (70 g) plaster of Paris
2/3 cup (150 ml) water
nail or pin
felt pens
measuring cups

leather thong
spoon
shellac, optional
wax paper
rag

Art Process

1. Mix one cup of plaster of Paris into two-thirds of a cup of water in a measuring cup with a spoon until thick and smooth. Remember to work fast because plaster hardens quickly.
2. Drop spoonfuls of plaster on the wax paper. Harden for five to ten minutes. If necessary, smooth plaster with the back of a spoon.
3. If a necklace is planned, poke a hole in the top of the plaster blob on the wax paper while the plaster is still soft.
4. When the plaster has hardened, scratch a design in the plaster with a nail or pin to etch a design just like the whalers did on shark tooth, whale bone and walrus tusk.
5. Draw on the scratched design with felt pens and then rub away the excess. The ink will fill the scratches.
6. Draw additional designs and pictures on the plaster, if desired.
7. Cover the pendant with shellac, if desired, to preserve the design.
8. Run a leather thong through the hole and wear the plaster scrimshaw as a pendant or necklace.

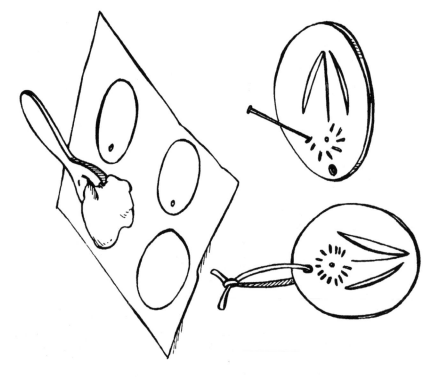

HINT · Young artists sometimes make very large pendants–VERY large–but enjoy wearing them anyway.

C
R
A
F
T

Winter

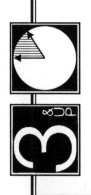

Cinnamon Drawing

Materials
cinnamon sticks
sandpaper
scissors

Art Process
1. Cut the sandpaper into any shapes or use as is.
2. Draw on the sandpaper with a cinnamon stick.

Variations
• Cut the sandpaper into holiday shapes and string on yarn with other decorations between each shape. You can use styrofoam peanuts, pieces of foil, pieces of colored paper or wrapping paper, playdough beads or other interesting items. Hang the garland from the ceiling around the room. Mmmmm, it smells nice too!
• Cut little squares of sandpaper and string a necklace on yarn. Punch holes with a paper punch in the small cinnamon squares of sandpaper. This makes a nice smelling necklace.
• Glue glitter or yarn to the edge of the sandpaper designs to decorate.

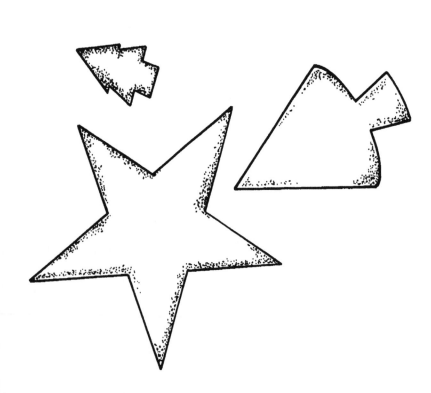

HINT
• Sandpaper is difficult to cut and can dull scissors.
• Young artists like to really scribble and scrub the cinnamon on the sandpaper for the fragrance more than the design.

D
R
A
W
I
N
G

Fabric Transfer

Materials

fabric crayons
white paper
fabric—old sheet, muslin, a T-shirt or pillowcase
old iron
pad of newspaper for ironing

Art Process

1. Draw or color heavily with fabric crayons on white paper.
   (Follow the directions on the fabric crayon box.)
2. Place the fabric on the pad of newspaper.
3. Place the drawing face down on the fabric.
4. **Adult** presses the paper with a warm iron using a firm straight
   down pressing motion rather than a traditional back and forth
   ironing motion. The picture from the fabric crayons will transfer
   to the fabric.
5. Remove the piece of paper with the fabric crayon design. The
   wax will have melted into the fabric and the heat will set the
   color into the fabric.

Variations

- Individual squares could be sewn into a quilt.
- Decorate a bandana, book bag, cloth napkins, table cloth or any
  other fabric idea.

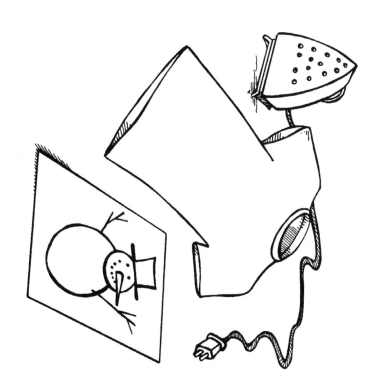

HINT

- Fabric crayons are available at all fabric and craft
  stores and often in art supply areas of stores that carry
  regular crayons.
- The drawing made with fabric crayon will not look
  like the drawings made with regular crayon but the
  transferred design will have bright and true colors.
  The colors may look different than regular crayons.
- As with any ironing project, an adult should either do the
  ironing or supervise older artists with the ironing.

Stained Glass Melt

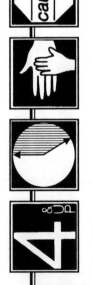

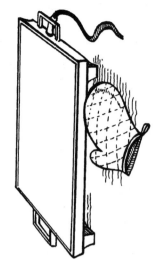

Materials
white paper
black felt pens
old crayons, peeled
warming tray
heavy glove or oven mitt
scissors and tape, optional

Art Process
1. Use the black felt pen to outline a design on the white paper. The blank spaces will be "colored in" with melted crayon.
2. Place the paper with black outlines and drawings on the warming tray.
3. Put a heavy glove or oven mitt on the non-drawing hand. Hold the paper down with this hand.
4. Using the peeled crayons, color in the pen design. Working slowly will allow the crayon to melt and soak into the paper.
5. Remove the design from the warming tray. Hold the paper up to the light or a window and see the stained glass effect.
6. The design can be cut out and displayed in a window to resemble a stained glass window.

Variations
- Artists can observe real stained glass windows which will enhance their imaginations as they create.
- Rub the back of the crayon design with a cotton ball soaked in baby oil for a more transparent design.

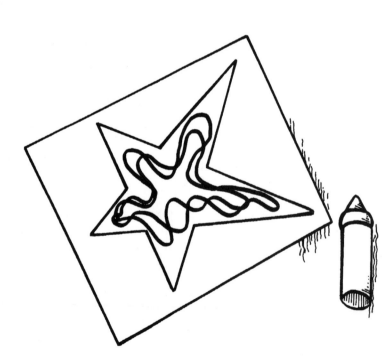

HINT
- As with any project involving heat or electricity, observe safety and caution. Tape the cord from the warming tray to the table and push the table against the wall.
- Some young artists will not have the concept of stained glass and will simply enjoy melting crayon in pretty but random experiments.

D R A W I N G

Peeled Glue

Materials

bottle of white glue
wax paper
felt pens
thread or yarn
newspaper to cover table

Art Process

1. Drip glue on a piece of wax paper in a design. Make thick masses, shapes or forms.
2. Dry the glue until hard and clear.
3. Decorate the dry glue shapes with felt pens.
4. Carefully peel the dry, decorated glue shapes off the wax paper.
5. The shapes can be laced with thread or yarn and hung from the ceiling, worn as jewelry or used as holiday decorations.

Variations

• Mix tempera paint into the glue for a colored glue.
• Sprinkle glitter or salt on the glue before it dries for a sparkling effect.

HINT
• Peeling the glue takes some patience and coordination so an adult may wish to help with this step.
• It may take several days until the glue dries clear and hard, depending on weather conditions.

DRAWING

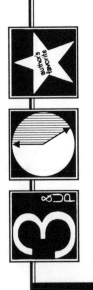

Paper Drop Dye

Materials

variety of papers—rice paper, coffee filter, blotting paper or
    paper towels
food coloring in several bowls
eyedroppers
newsprint to cover table

Art Process

1. Cover the table with newsprint.
2. Place a piece of absorbent paper on the newsprint.
3. Fill an eyedropper with color from one bowl and drop a spot of color onto the paper.
4. Use another eyedropper to add another color. The colors will blend to make a pattern.
5. Transfer the paper to a clean piece of newsprint to dry.

Variations

- When the project is dry, paper can be cut into a snowflake design, used as wrapping paper or hung in a window to enjoy the bright colors.
- Fold and dip the paper into the bowls of color instead of using the eyedroppers.
- Use powdered paint or fabric dye available from art stores instead of food coloring. Although these dyes seem expensive, they last a long time, go a long way and come in an amazing rainbow of bright colors.

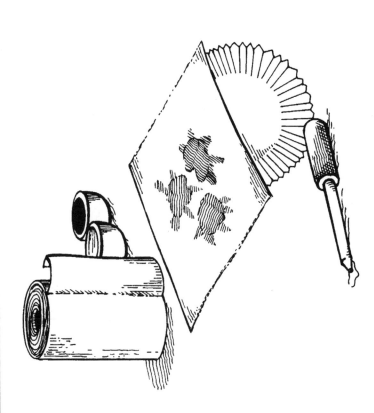

HINT
- Many young artists become absorbed in the blending of colors and end up with a substantially soaked piece of paper which can be difficult to move. Work on a sheet of newsprint sturdy enough to hold the finished artwork that can be lifted and carried to a drying location.
- Expect fingers and hands to be stained. The color can take several days to wash out. Protect clothing with an old shirt or smock.

PAINTING

Shiny Painting

Materials

Paint mixture: liquid tempera paint for color, 4 tablespoons corn
syrup, 1-1/2 teaspoons liquid dishwashing soap
matte board or cardboard
paint brushes
mixing spoons
small containers

Art Process

1. Make the paint mixture of liquid tempera paint, corn syrup and
dishwashing soap. Place the paint in small containers.
2. Paint freely with the mixture using any painting approach on
matte board or cardboard for a sturdy base.

Variations

· Dip string or yarn into the Shiny Paint and press between sheets
of paper for a shiny yarn design. Then, remove yarn.
· Place paper in a baking pan and roll marbles through puddles of
Shiny Paint.
· Use the Shiny Paint on white or colored tissue paper to create
wrapping paper.

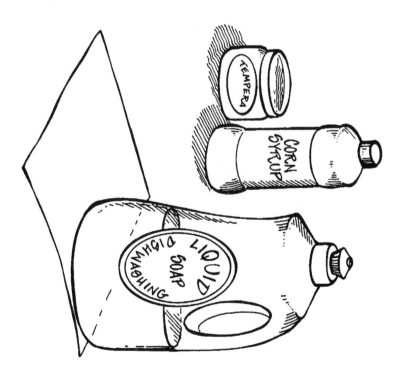

HINT · This paint is very pretty and glossy which makes it
nice for holiday themes.

· This paint is also very sticky and dries slower than
regular paint

PAINTING

Insole Stamps

Materials
shoe insoles
pen
scissors
rubber cement
wooden block scrap
ink pad or paint spread on paper towels

Art Process
1. Draw a design on the latex side (not the fabric side) of the insole.
2. Cut out the design with scissors.
3. Glue the cutout shape to a scrap of wood with rubber cement.
4. When dry, press the block stamp into a regular ink pad. (If no ink pads are available, spread some paint or food coloring on a pad of paper towels in a styrofoam tray and use like an ink pad.)

Variations
· The insole shape can be glued to a jar lid or a piece of heavy cardboard.
· Use this idea for decorating holiday wrapping paper or making greeting cards.

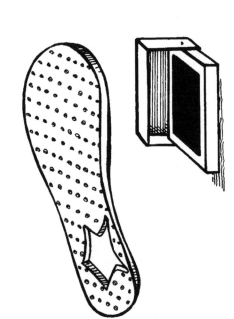

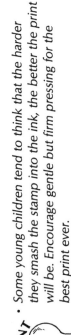

HINT · Some young children tend to think that the harder they smash the stamp into the ink, the better the print will be. Encourage gentle but firm pressing for the best print ever.

· Other glues will also work if rubber cement is not available or objectionable due to the odor or fumes it emits.

P A I N T I N G

Stained Glass Painting

Materials

white drawing paper
permanent black marking pen
bright liquid tempera paints in cups
paint brushes

Art Process

1. Draw bold black lines on the paper using the marking pen.
2. Paint inside the lines with the bright tempera paints.

Variations

- For a shiny paint, see Shiny Painting (p.119) for this project.
- Paint black lines with black tempera paint. When dry, fill in the black lines with bright tempera paints.

HINT · Permanent pens soak through paper and can stain the table so cover the table with plastic or newsprint. Any marks on the table can be removed with powdered cleanser. To remove pen marks from clothes, spray the stain with hair spray, rinse, spray again and, rinse again. Continue this pattern until the stain is completely gone.

· Some people prefer not to use permanent pens with young children due to the fumes from the ink. The decision is yours.

PAINTING

Snow Paint

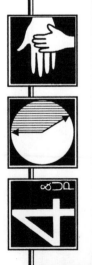

Materials

dark construction paper such as purple and blue
crayons
paintbrushes
4 tablespoons Epsom salt
1/4 cup (60 ml) hot water
small cups or bowls
spoons
covered table

Art Process

1. Mix one-quarter cup hot water with four tablespoons of Epsom salt. Stir the mixture to dissolve.
2. Draw freely with the crayons on the dark construction paper.
3. Brush the drawing with the salt mixture.
4. Dry the painting completely.

Variation

· Cut snowy designs from the paper and hang with string.

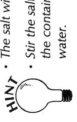

HINT
· The salt will dry to a snowy, crystal effect.
· Stir the salt water each time a brush is dipped into the container to keep the brush full of very salty water.
· The salt crystals brush off the paper when dry.
· Table salt or rock salt can be substituted for Epsom salt

P A I N T I N G

Window Painting

Materials
paintbrushes
newspapers
tape
liquid tempera paints in containers

Art Process
1. Tape newspaper to the bottom edges of windows to protect floors and ledges.
2. Paint on the inside of the window so rain will not wash off the painting.
3. Leave the design on the windows for days or weeks.
4. Wash the design off with a sponge and soapy water. (This is a messy job!)

Variations
- Paint holiday scenes or designs or use holiday colors to paint any designs.
- Cover the window with a large sheet of cellophane and paint on the cellophane instead of the window.
- Paint with white shoe polish and the applicators which come in the polish bottles. This is very easy to clean up. White is nice for snow scenes, too.

HINT
- Mix powdered tempera paint with liquid dishwashing soap and water for easier removal.
- Mix paint with white shoe polish for optional easy removal.
- The longer the paint is left on the window, the harder it is to remove.

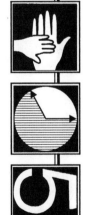

P
A
I
N
T
I
N
G

Sugar Mint Modeling

Materials

Dough Mixture:

1/3 cup (70 g) butter or margarine
1/3 cup (75 ml) light corn syrup
1 teaspoon peppermint extract
1/2 teaspoon salt
1 lb. (450 g) powdered sugar (1 box)

food coloring
large bowl
small bowls
spoons

Art Process

1. Be sure hands are clean before beginning this activity.
2. Mix all the ingredients except the food coloring in a large bowl.
3. Divide the mixture into separate small bowls, one for each color desired.
4. With a spoon, stir drops of food coloring into each bowl.
5. With clean hands, create designs and sculptures with the sugar mint mixture. Combine and mix colors too.
6. Sugar Mint Sculptures are edible but are very very sweet.

Variation

- Experiment with other flavorings such as almond, vanilla or lemon instead of mint.

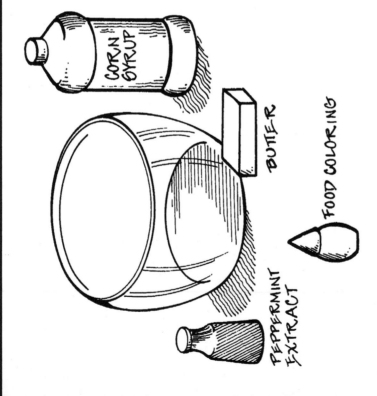

CORN SYRUP

BUTTER

FOOD COLORING

PEPPERMINT EXTRACT

HINT
- Fingers and faces get sticky (surprise!) so have water and towels available. Also, warm little hands can soften the dough substantially; this is when things start to get sticky.

- Sculptures can be refrigerated. They will harden somewhat. Give the finished sculptures as gifts wrapped in cellophane or plastic wrap and tied with a bow. Artists may want to eat their creation right on the spot

DOUGH

Bread Sculpture

Materials

1 tablespoon or 1 pkg dry yeast
1 cup (230 ml) water
1 teaspoon sugar
2 cups (400 g) flour
1 tablespoon oil
400 degree oven
cooling rack
kitchen tools for modeling
(knife, fork, toothpick)

1 teaspoon salt
mixing bowl
wooden spoon
clean towel

Art Process

1. Wash hands before beginning. Mix the water, sugar and yeast in a bowl until the yeast softens (about two to three minutes).
2. Add one cup of flour and stir vigorously with a wooden spoon. Beat the mixture until smooth and add one tablespoon of oil and one teaspoon of salt. Next add the second cup of flour to the dough.
3. Pour the thick batter onto a floured board and add more flour slowly while kneading the dough. Keep a coating of flour on the dough to prevent sticking.
4. Knead for about five minutes. The dough should be smooth, elastic and satiny and should bounce back if a finger is poked into it. Place the dough in an oiled bowl and cover with a clean towel. Set the bowl in a warm place for dough to rise for about forty-five minutes.
5. Punch the dough down and work it into a smooth ball. Divide the dough into portions for various parts of the bread sculpture or for different children to use.

6. Create sculptures with the dough. Create any shapes or designs.
7. Bake the sculptures for fifteen or twenty minutes in the lower part of a 400 degree oven. Large forms may take longer. Bake until golden and baked through. Cool the sculptures on a rack. Eat and enjoy.

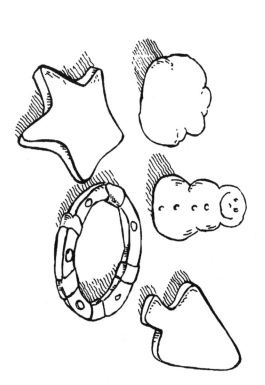

HINT

- Bread dough sculptures work well for holidays.
- Young artists like to keep a small bowl of flour handy to keep their hands powdery while working. Sometimes they like the soft flour better than the sculptures.

author's favorite

caution

4
PC&8

D O U G H

Marzipan Fantasy Fruits

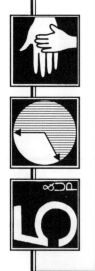

Materials

marzipan
food coloring
cloves
sliced almonds
clean work surface
airtight containers or plastic wrap

Art Process

1. Wash hands before beginning. Break marzipan into several balls, one ball for each color of fantasy fruit.
2. Add a little food coloring to each ball and work the coloring into the marzipan with hands.
3. Using the colored marzipan, create real fruits, imaginary fruits or any shapes and designs.
4. Add sliced almonds for leaves and cloves for stems to the designs.
5. Store marzipan fantasy fruits in airtight containers or with plastic wrap.
6. Fruits are edible, however, most children don't seem to like the flavor of marzipan.

Variations

- Make sculptures other than fruits such as balloons, clowns, animals, flowers or abstract shapes.
- Use this project as gifts for the holidays.

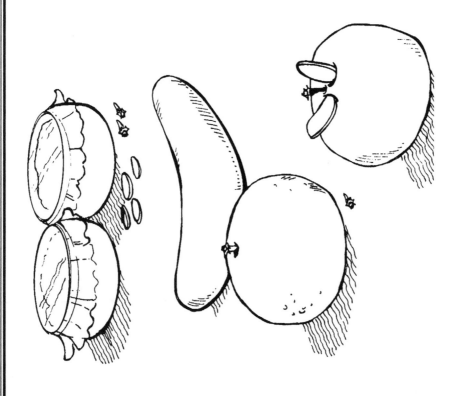

HINT
- Marzipan is available from bakeries, grocery stores, candy stores and cake baking supply stores.

DOUGH

Royal Icing Art

Materials

1-1/4 cups (250 g) powdered sugar
1 egg white at room temperature
1/2 teaspoon lemon juice
egg beater or electric mixer
small bowl
yummy decorations including candies, cookies, sweets, marshmallows, sprinkles or shredded coconut
pipe cleaners
spreading knives
foil covered cardboard or a pizza cardboard circle

Art Process

1. An adult should beat the egg white until stiff.
2. Add sifted powdered sugar a tablespoon at a time, beating after each addition.
3. When the icing is a thick spreading consistency, add the lemon juice which helps with quick drying.
4. Work on the foil covered cardboard or pizza circle. Use the icing as cement or glue and stick cookies and sweets together to make animals, toys, or holiday scenes.
5. Eat right away or display for all to see and enjoy.

Variation

- Make little cookie houses; a barnyard scene with a marshmallow pig and cookie fence; a Santa face with white icing beard and jelly bean nose; a ski scene with toy skiers on icing hills or other creative ideas.

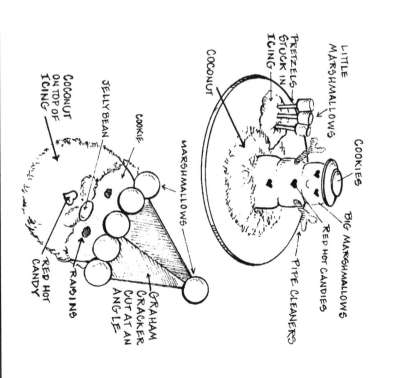

LITTLE MARSHMALLOWS
COOKIES
PRETZELS STUCK IN ICING
COCONUT
BIG MARSHMALLOWS
RED HOT CANDIES
PIPE CLEANERS
MARSHMALLOWS
COCONUT ON TOP OF ICING
JELLYBEAN
COOKIE
RAISINS
RED HOT CANDY
GRAHAM CRACKER CUT AT AN ANGLE

HINT

- As with any edible activity, wash hands before beginning.
- Royal Icing can be doubled, tripled or made in any quantity. However, for large batches, keep a damp cloth over the bowl to prevent the icing from drying out.
- Excess icing can be stored in airtight containers in the refrigerator for up to a week.

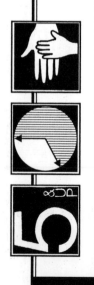

Candy Bugs

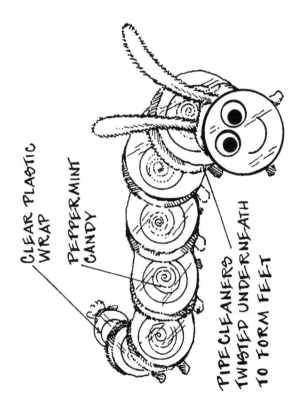

CLEAR PLASTIC WRAP

PEPPERMINT CANDY

PIPE CLEANERS TWISTED UNDERNEATH TO FORM FEET

Materials

clear plastic wrap
colored pipe cleaners
ribbons, rubber bands and string
small candy pieces
dried fruits such as apricots
toothpicks

Art Process

1. Place candy pieces on a strip of plastic wrap and wind the plastic wrap around them to form a caterpillar or other insect shapes.
2. Twist pipe cleaners between pieces of candy or at appropriate intervals to form the head, body and legs. Use rubber bands, string or ribbons too.
3. Candy Bugs make delicious treats or great party favors for birthdays.

Variation

- Toothpicks can be stuck into the bug for spines, antennae, stingers or teeth.

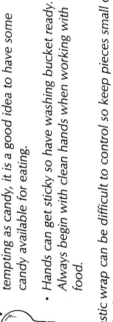

HINT
- Any time you are working with something as tempting as candy, it is a good idea to have some candy available for eating.
- Hands can get sticky so have washing bucket ready. Always begin with clean hands when working with food.
- Plastic wrap can be difficult to control so keep pieces small or help the young artist with the wrap.

S C U L P T U R E

String Ornaments

Materials

various lengths of string or embroidery floss
white glue, thinned with water in a small bowl
wax paper
glitter
scissors
wet towel for clean up

Art Process

1. Dip the string in the thinned glue.
2. Wipe excess glue off the string by pulling it through the pointer finger and thumb or by pulling it across the edge of the bowl. (Be ready to clean fingers with the wet towel.)
3. Place the string on the wax paper in any shape, design, pattern or form.
4. Sprinkle glitter over the string.
5. Dry the string design completely.
6. Gently peel the string design off of the wax paper.
7. Hang the string as an ornament if desired.

Variations

• Make definite shapes such as circles, stars, diamonds or other designs with the string.
• Add tempera paint to the thinned glue for a colored glue.
• Sprinkle other things on the ornaments such as colored sand, confetti or candy sprinkles.

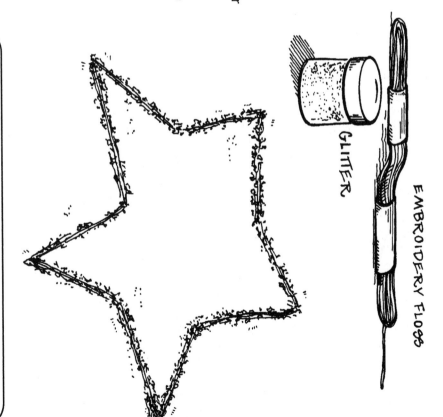

GLITTER

EMBROIDERY FLOSS

HINT

• This project will need to dry at least overnight
• Peeling the string from the wax paper can be tricky.

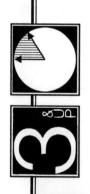

Tile Marking

Materials
white ceramic tiles
permanent felt markers
apron

Art Process
1. Draw on white ceramic tiles with permanent markers.
2. Tiles dry quickly.

Variations
- Use decorated tiles for trivets or hot pads to protect the table from hot dishes or foods.
- Tiles make nice gifts.
- Decorate the tiles with holiday themes for holiday gifts or decorations.

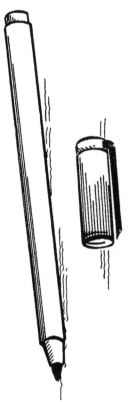

HINT
- Free tiles can be collected from contractors who have leftover tiles or contact a local home design store for tile samples or leftovers.
- Pens can stain so prepare by covering the table, child or anything in the work area which could possibly be damaged.

Light Holes

Materials
black paper
heavy cardboard for work surface
poking tools such as a pencil, nail, pin, bamboo skewer or scissors
tape
glue
scraps of colored tissue, cellophane and colored paper

Art Process
1. Tape a square of black paper to the cardboard work surface.
2. Use the poking tools to punch holes in the black paper. Make as many holes in as many sizes as desired.
3. Remove the tape.
4. Cover the holes with any colored paper by gluing or taping the papers on the back of the black paper. It is pretty to cover each hole or a few holes with small scraps of tissue or cellophane.
5. Place the Light Holes design in a window or hold it up to the light to see the colored lights.

Variations
• Make holes in a pattern or design.
• Work on black paper that has been cut into a pattern such as a tree, star or circle.
• Poke holes in colored paper and tape the paper to a sheet of black paper. The holes seem to "pop out" using this method.
• Glue the poked paper on a sheet of foil for shiny holes.
• Use a piece of plywood for the work surface and make all the holes using a hammer and nails.

HINT
• When working with sharp tools supervise closely. Allow plenty of room between artists and set a rule that all sharp objects must be left on the table if the artist must get up for any reason.
• Some artists have not learned to control poking holes through paper. The paper can tear rather than making a hole. Paper tears can be taped on the back or may be incorporated into the final design.

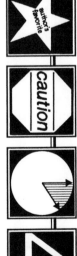

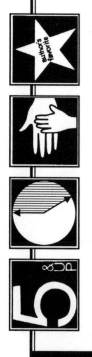

Photo Sculpture

Materials

magazine picture or photograph
foam core board (art store)
white glue (thinned with water in a dish) or rubber cement (as is)
brush for glue
scissors
2 picture frame scraps, equal lengths
tape or rubber bands
glue gun, optional

Art Process

1. Carefully cut out a good sized photograph or magazine picture for the sculpture.
2. Place the picture on the foam core board and trace the outline. Remove the picture. **Adult** cuts the foam core on the traced line.
3. Glue the picture to the foam core being careful to stick the edges down and smooth out wrinkles.
4. Dry the picture completely.
5. Trim any excess picture or foam core if necessary.
6. For the base, put glue on the inside edges of two frame scraps. Place the photo sculpture upright between the frame pieces and press them together with the photograph between them. Hold the frames together using tape or rubber bands until dry.
7. For magazine picture sculptures, paint a coat of white glue over the entire sculpture including the frame scrap base and all the edges of the foam core.

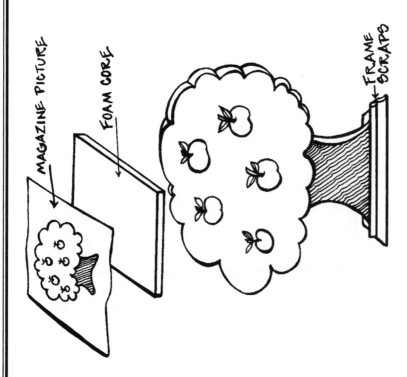

MAGAZINE PICTURE
FOAM CORE
FRAME SCRAPS

HINT
· Sometimes the glue leaks down between the wood scraps and the photo sculpture ends up stuck to the table. To prevent this from happening, move the sculptures often or dry them on a baker's cooling rack or wire mesh screen. Lift the sculptures when dry.

· The photo sculpture has a life-like look when displayed.

Advent Boxes

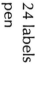

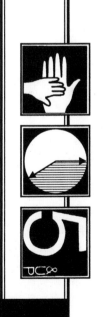

Materials

24 small boxes (jewelry or match boxes)
holiday wrapping paper scraps
ribbon
tape
sweets, nuts or small toys
24 labels
pen
scissors

Art Process

1. Fill each box with sweets, nuts or small toys.
2. Wrap each box with wrapping paper scraps.
3. Tie each box with ribbon. Curl ends of ribbons if desired.
4. Label each box with numbers from one to twenty four.
5. Cut twenty four long pieces of ribbon and tie one to each box.
6. Adjust the way the boxes hang so they hang at different lengths.
7. Gather all the ribbons in one hand at the top, divide them into two bunches and tie the two bunches together in a knot or bow. Add an even larger bow to the top of the advent box hanging, if desired.
8. Hang up the advents boxes and open one box each day starting on the first of December. The twenty fourth box will be opened on the day before Christmas.

Variation

• Other ideas for things to put in each box include: wishes for others, little drawings or pictures of holiday things or greetings from holiday cards.

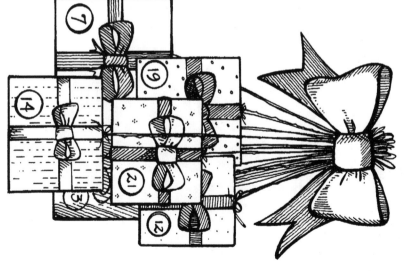

HINT

• *Most of this activity is adult assisted. The fun for the child is opening the boxes each day. Wrapping the boxes is something children can do, but keep in mind that they don't do it the way adults would.*

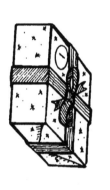

C R A F T

5

PC8

Chalk Dip

Materials
colored chalk
1 tablespoon thick, white tempera paint
jar lid
black or dark paper

Art Process
1. Dip the end of a piece of colored chalk into some thick white tempera paint in a jar lid.
2. Draw with the whitened, moist chalk. The marks will show the distinct color of the chalk edged with white tempera against the dark paper.

Variations
- Make a sampler of markings such as zigzags, spirals, curves, straight lines and other markings on dark paper.
- Experiment with dipping the chalk in black paint and then working on white paper.

HINT
- Scrubbing with the tempera-dipped chalk creates a mixed, blurry tint instead of the color edged in white.
- Chalk can blur and smudge on hands, clothes and on the paper. This is a natural occurrence when mixing chalk and young children.

D
R
A
W
I
N
G

Glue and Chalk Draw

Materials

white glue in squeeze bottle
colored chalk
dark paper
hair spray as a fixative, optional

Art Process

1. Draw a freeform design on dark paper with glue.
2. Dry the glue overnight.
3. Apply colored chalk to the areas between the clear glue lines. The glue lines will appear to be black and the chalk will have a muted effect on the other areas.
4. An **adult** can spray the chalk and glue drawing with a fixative if desired. Hair spray works well. Spray the artwork outside or in a well ventilated area away from the children.

Variations

· Draw with glue on white paper, dry and then paint the spaces between the glue lines. The lines will appear white.

· An adult can add black India ink to the glue. Follow the same steps on white or black paper, using watercolors or chalk to fill in the spaces.

HINT
· The black paper dulls the chalk so it has a muted effect.

· Chalk is always messy for young artists; this is to be expected and enjoyed. Have warm, soapy water handy for clean-up.

Little Art Books

Materials

light scrap paper or newsprint (cut in 3 or 4 strips about 3" x 8")
heavy paper for the book cover, 3" x 8" (6 cm x 20 cm)
stapler, brads, yarn or pipe cleaners for binding
crayons or markers

Art Process

1. **Adult** folds three to four strips of scrap paper in half.
2. **Adult** adds a cover to the strips. Staple the entire booklet together or use some other form of binding. The booklet can be put together using hole punches and yarn, brads or pipe cleaners.
3. The artist can draw pictures or designs on each page.
4. Decorate the cover.

Variations

- Use three by five inch index cards stapled together.
- Make little art books with different colors of paper and set out different types of drawing materials such as colored pencils, stencils, a ruler and tape.

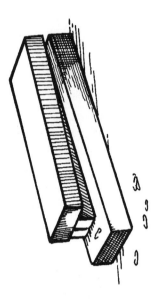

MY LITTLE ART BOOK
SUZY

HINT
- Young artists can make their own books after they have been shown how. Staplers are fascinating to young artists so be prepared for a substantially stapled creation.
- If the artist has a title for the book, offer to write it on the front along with any other writing or dictation the artist might like on each page too.

DRAWING

Zigzag Gallery

Materials

2 pieces of cardboard for the cover, 8" x 10" (20 cm x 25 cm)
matte board or posterboard cut in 8" x 10" pieces for the pages
masking tape or cloth library tape
crayons, pens

Art Process

1. Draw a series of pictures or designs which tell a story. Pictures may also be a collection of thoughts or designs based on one theme or topic. You may also use a collection of favorite drawings.
2. An adult should tape the matte boards together with masking tape or cloth library tape so that the pages fold in an accordion style.
3. Add the cardboard covers with tape.
4. Fold the zigzag book into a book shape or display the opened gallery on a table or shelf.

Variations

- Cut out shapes from paper or wall paper scraps and paste the shapes on each matte board instead of drawing.
- Illustrate a favorite story or fairy tale.
- Make a zigzag book that has no sequence or collection of thoughts but is simply a collection of artwork, drawings and designs.

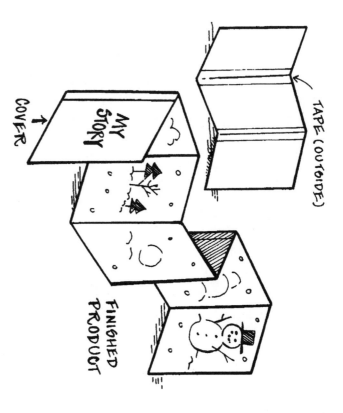

TAPE (OUTSIDE)

COVER

MY STORY

FINISHED PRODUCT

HINT

- The taping of the pages together is definitely an adult step.
- Sequence can be a bit abstract for very young artists, but this project can help make sense out of it.
- Cutting the matte boards in a square, say ten by ten inches, eliminates the problem of drawings being sideways in the finished product
- Library fabric tape comes in many colors from school supply stores and works well in place of the masking tape.

Snowy Etching

Materials

crayons

white drawing paper, any size

scraping tool such as a blunt pencil, scissors point, paper clip or spoon

Art Process

1. Using muscles and determination, completely color a piece (or a section) of white drawing paper. Color hard and shiny using various colors of blue, white and gray crayons.
2. Using black or dark blue, color over the first layer of colors.
3. When complete, scratch a design of a snowman, a snowy day, snowflakes or any other design into the top layer of crayon. The first layer will show through.

Variations

- Instead of a second layer of crayon, use white or black paint over the first layer of crayon. Then finger paint in the paint. The slick, shiny crayon background will act like finger painting paper.
- Color a square, circle or other shape in the center of the paper, reducing the challenge of coloring such a large area.

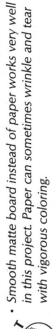

HINT · Smooth matte board instead of paper works very well in this project. Paper can sometimes wrinkle and tear with vigorous coloring.

· Recommended for artists with enough patience and muscular strength to color a thick layer over a full sheet of paper. Not all artists should be expected to work at this pace or intensity.

D
R
A
W
I
N
G

Five Block Prints

Materials

5 printing materials: 1. insulation tape (peel-off variety), 2. styrofoam grocery tray, 3. felt scraps, 4. cardboard strips and 5. string

5 wooden blocks

white glue in squeeze bottle

scissors

tempera paint

old washcloth

water

cookie sheet

paper

Art Process

1. Cut each of the five printing materials into shapes or patterns
   and glue each one to a block of wood. (The insulation tape will
   stick on its own.) Allow the glue to dry.
2. Meanwhile, dampen an old washcloth in water and wring it out.
3. Place it on a cookie sheet.
4. Spread tempera paint on the damp washcloth to be used as the
   stamp pad.
5. Press a dry woodblock design into the paint and then press it
   onto the paper.
6. Combine different print designs or make patterns using only
   one block per piece of paper.

Variations

- Use food coloring, paste food coloring, dye, inks or ink pads for
  the printing step instead of paint.
- Make wrapping paper by printing on a large sheets of white
  tissue.

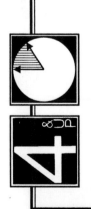

Palette Painting

Materials

thick finger paint, many colors in muffin tins or cups
palette knife, plastic knife, craft stick or tongue depressor
matte board or cardboard
covered table

Art Process

1. Using a palette knife or palette knife substitute, spread paint on the matte board surface in the same way that butter is spread on toast.
2. Experiment with the end and sides of the knife for other effects.
3. Dry the artwork overnight.

Variation

- Use other tools for spreading, mixing and painting such as a cotton swab, pencil, stick, spatula or spoon.

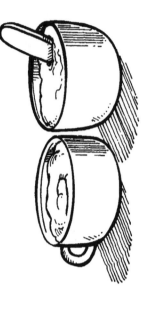

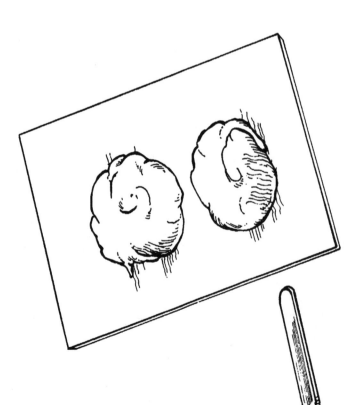

HINT · Palette knife painting enables the artist to see how colors mix, to experiment with stroke and design and to feel the thickness of paint and how it can be manipulated. Many young artists end up with something resembling chocolate mud on their matte board but this just shows how much they have enjoyed and experimented with color mixing. Give them another matte board. Each experiment will yield a new appreciation and result.

P A I N T I N G

Swinging Paint

Materials

masking tape
large paper
paintbrushes in a variety of sizes
string
tempera paint, in a variety of colors in trays or cans

Art Process

1. Tape a large sheet of paper to the floor.
2. Next tie strings to the handles of a variety of paintbrushes.
3. Dip the paintbrush into the paint.
4. While standing over the paper, hold the string and let the paintbrush hang down and touch the paper. Swing the paintbrush making designs as the brush dangles, swings and brushes against the paper.
5. Refill brushes with paint as needed.

Variation

- Hang other objects from strings such as a cotton swab, pencil, nuts, bolts or eraser. Dip these items in the paint and make designs on the paper with them.

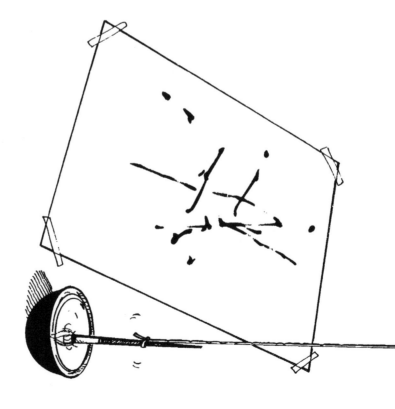

HINT • The brushes are a bit hard to control with drips and so forth. Protect the floor with plastic or newsprint.

4

P
A
I
N
T
I
N
G

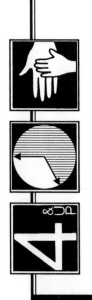

Easy Pendulum Paint

Materials

small plastic funnel
strong string
tape
large sheet of paper

powdered tempera paint
liquid starch
scissors
small pitcher

Art Process

1. An adult should tie a string around the large edge of a plastic funnel. Tie or tape three strings about fifteen inches in length spaced equally around the edge of the funnel. Tie the three ends together above the funnel.
2. Mix liquid starch and powdered tempera paint in a pitcher so that it flows smoothly, but is not too thin.
3. Hold the pendulum funnel and string over the paper.
4. Place a finger over the spout of the funnel with the other hand.
5. **Adult** pours paint into the funnel.
6. When the funnel is full, remove the finger and give the funnel a swing.
7. Keep the pendulum funnel moving until all the paint has run out of the funnel.
8. Add a new color to the funnel and keep painting, if desired.

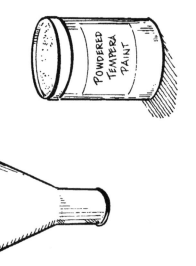

Variations

- Balance a dowel from one chair to another and hang the pendulum funnel from the dowel. Proceed as above by adding paint and removing the finger from the spout to release the paint.
- Fill the funnel with colored sand, plain sand or salt and dry tempera paint mixed together. Proceed as above.

HINT · This project takes some coordination and timing but is great fun and creates very interesting designs.

P A I N T I N G

Paste Batik

Materials

1/2 cup (100 g) flour
1/2 cup (100 ml) water
2 teaspoons alum
blender
small piece of 100% cotton muslin, unlaundered
corrugated cardboard
several squeeze bottles
paste food color from cake decorating store
several clean empty shallow cans
paintbrushes

tape
water
scissors
iron

Art Process

1. Mix the first three ingredients into a paste using a blender. Put some of the paste in several squeeze bottles.

2. Tape the muslin to a square of cardboard. Draw with the squeeze bottles of paste on the muslin. Try to maintain a smooth flow of paste. Dots, lines and solid masses are also effective. Dry the project overnight.

3. Mix paste food colors in shallow tin cans with water. A small amount will give a rich hue.

4. Dip a paintbrush into the food color mixture and brush colors over the dry paste designs. Dry the project completely.

5. Chip and rub the dry paste off the muslin with fingers. The drawing underneath will be white.

Variation

· Make a greeting card by gluing the batik to a piece of colored paper.

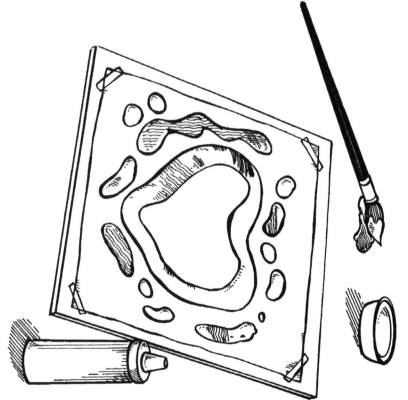

HINT
· Shallow tuna or pineapple cans are more stable than tall containers for the paste food coloring.
· A large three by five foot piece of muslin would work well for a group project.

Salt Figures

Materials

salt ceramic clay mixture: one cup (200 g) salt, 1/2 cup (100 g) cornstarch and 3/4 cup (150 g) water

saucepan and wooden spoon

stove

cardboard tube or empty frozen juice can

large ball of salt ceramic clay

small balls of salt ceramic clay colored with food coloring

toothpicks

decorating materials such as yarn, cotton, felt, colored paper, scraps of fabric, feathers, fabric trims or lace

glue or tape

Art Process

1. **Adult** cooks the clay ingredients over medium heat in a saucepan. Stir with a wooden spoon until the mixture thickens into a ball. Remove from the heat and place on a piece of foil to cool. Knead the dough thoroughly.
2. Fill the tube with clay or something else heavy enough to keep it from tipping over.
3. Place a ball of clay on top of the tube for a head. Add other bits of colored clay for facial features. If features won't stick, moisten the clay with a bit of water and then attach. Toothpicks also help features stick to the clay.
4. Dry for several days until the heads and tube fillings are dry.
5. Add any decorations for clothing, hair, hats, glasses, beards, arms or braids. Use glue or tape.

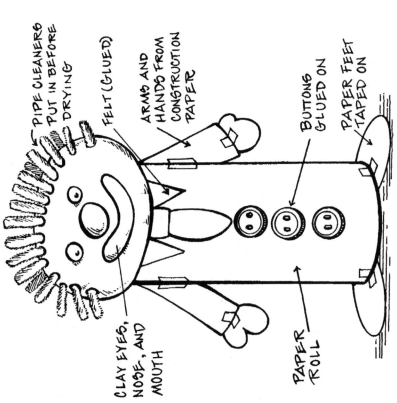

PIPE CLEANERS PUT IN BEFORE DRYING

FELT (GLUED)

ARMS AND HANDS FROM CONSTRUCTION PAPER

CLAY EYES, NOSE, AND MOUTH

BUTTONS GLUED ON

PAPER FEET TAPED ON

PAPER ROLL

HINT
- Salt ceramic clay often needs to be re-kneaded to make it smooth and pliable again.
- Clay can be stored in an airtight plastic bag until ready to use.
- Salt ceramic dries to a rock hardness without being baked.

C
L
A
Y

Wire Sculpting

Materials

plaster of Paris
water
measuring cups
bowl
spoon
1/2 pint individual milk carton
scrap telephone cable (colored wires inside the cable) pre-cut to
   12" or other manageable lengths
watercolor paints, optional
decorative items such as beads or ribbon, optional

Art Process

1. **Adult** mixes one cup of plaster of Paris with one-half cup of
   water in a bowl with a spoon. (Note: Do not rinse plaster down
   the sink as it may harden in the pipes.)
2. Pour plaster into the small milk carton. (There will be enough
   plaster for about three cartons.)
3. As plaster begins to harden, the artist can place wires in the
   plaster in any fashion, any number and any arrangement. Dry
   the plaster until hard.
4. When plaster is dry and hard, tear away the milk carton. Bend
   and sculpt the wires into a shape or sculpture.
5. Add optional sculpture items to the wires if desired such as
   beads, ribbons or other items.
6. Plaster may be painted with watercolors or left white.

HINT

· Telephone cable can be collected from telephone
  installation representatives or call the local phone
  company to arrange pickup of scrap wire. The outer
  covering of the cable can be stripped away revealing
  a rainbow of wires which can be cut with scissors and
  used for many art experiences.

· Let plaster harden in the mixing bowl, pop it out when dry
  and then wipe the bowl with a wet towel. The bowl may be
  washed in the sink. Hands should be washed in a bucket of
  soapy water rather than in the sink. Throw the water outside.
  Never rinse plaster down the drain because it can harden in
  the plumbing and cause real trouble.

Collection Collage

Materials

assorted collage materials including pipe cleaners, crepe paper, paper muffin cups, stickers, foil, magazine pages, fabrics, notions, brads, feathers and yarn

white glue in cups with brushes

background material such as matte board, cardboard, wood or heavy paper

Art Process

1. Glue any assortment of collage items on the background materials.
2. Dip the brush in the cup of glue and paint the background surface; attach the object in the glue and add additional glue if necessary.
3. Form a realistic picture or a random design.

Variation

- Limit choices of material. For example, choose one decorating material and an interesting background material such as feathers on a grass cloth wallpaper, pompoms on colorful fabric or yarn scraps on bright matte board.

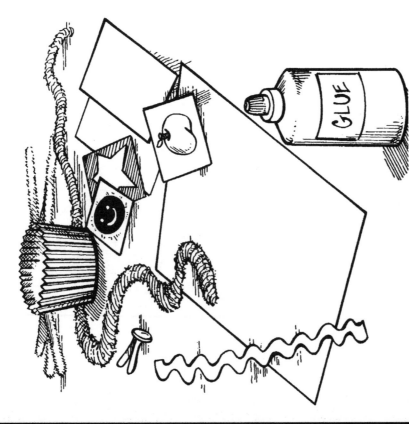

HINT • Stay out of the way during this project and watch the wonderful creativity of young artists.

Candle Holder

Materials
homemade playdough
small pine cones, weeds, sticks, seed pods and nuts
candle
aluminum pie plate
glitter
silver or gold spray paint, optional
bobby pins
ribbons

Art Process
1. Playdough will form the base of the candle holder. Place a ball of playdough in the pie plate and press it down to fill the plate.
2. Push a candle into the center of the playdough. The fat pillar candle varieties work well.
3. Push other items into the playdough such as pine cones, weeds, sticks, seed pods and nuts.
4. If a silver or gold candle holder is desired, remove the candle and an **adult** sprays the candle holder outside with silver or gold paint. Glitter may be sprinkled into the wet paint. When the base is dry, replace the candle.
5. Tie ribbons or bows to bobby pins and push the pin into the playdough too.
6. With adult supervision, light the candle briefly and then snuff out. Never burn candles unattended because the materials in this project are flammable.

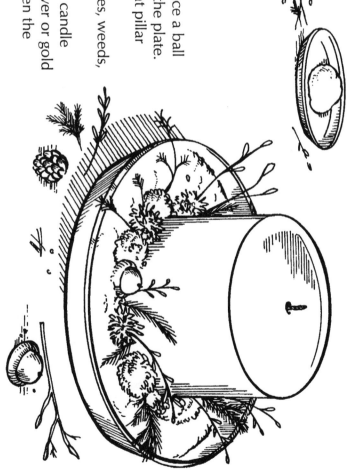

HINT • One-on-one adult supervision is necessary during the entire time the candle is lit.
• A safer variation is to set a votive candle inside a small clear jar and place this in the playdough candle holder. The glass jar will help contain the flame.

caution

3
8

C
R
A
F
T

Stuffed Fabric

Materials
pencil or crayon
plain or patterned fabric squares, about 8" (20 cm) square
scissors
fabric pens
fabric glue
stapler
pillow stuffing or scraps for stuffing
pinking shears

Art Process
1. Draw a design or shape on the fabric. Repeat the exact design.
2. Cut the shapes out with scissors.
3. Decorate the fabric with fabric pens, if desired.
4. Place the two undecorated identical shapes together, insides of fabric touching (right sides out).
5. Use fabric glue in a bottle to glue the edges together keeping one area open for stuffing. Dry the project completely or overnight.
6. Stuff the shape with fabric scraps or pillow stuffing.
7. When stuffed, glue the remaining edge of the shape. If it won't hold, staple that edge and remove staples when glue has dried.
8. Trim with a pinking shear or scalloping scissors after sealing with glue and stuffing.

FABRIC

DRAW AND CUT DESIGN OUT

GLUED AREA (STEP 4)

LAST (STEP 8) TRIM WITH PINKING SHEARS

STUFF AND GLUE CLOSED (STEP 7)

HINT
- Fabric glues are often very different in nature. Find one that says "Fast Drying" or "Good for Seams."
- Make stuffed toys, tree decorations or little dolls for big dolls to play with.
- Sew the shape on a machine or by hand instead of gluing.

Stuffed Stuff

Materials

scraps of butcher paper about 1 yard (1 m) square
newspaper or other large scrap paper
pens, crayon, paint and brushes
stapler
scissors
yarn

Art Process

1. Choose a shape or a design such as a fish, pumpkin, animal or abstract shape.
2. Draw it very large on a sheet of butcher paper.
3. An adult or the artist can cut out the shape from the outline. To make two shapes at once, staple two sheets together and then cut them at the same time. There will be two separate shapes.
4. Paint, draw or otherwise decorate both sides of the shape with colors or glue additional items to decorate.
5. Staple the two sheets together at the edge. Leave an opening on one of the sides of the shape.
6. Now stuff the shape with bunched up newspaper or other scraps of paper to fill out the shape. When filled, staple the closing.
7. Add yarn, if desired, to hang the Stuffed Stuff from the ceiling.

Variations

· Stuff the shape with a gift, prizes, candy, rewards or other fun items. Give this project to someone special.
· Make an entire zoo, undersea world or crazy shape garden out of Stuffed Stuff.

HINT · Young artists love large artwork. The stapling can be difficult, but allow the artist to do as much as possible.

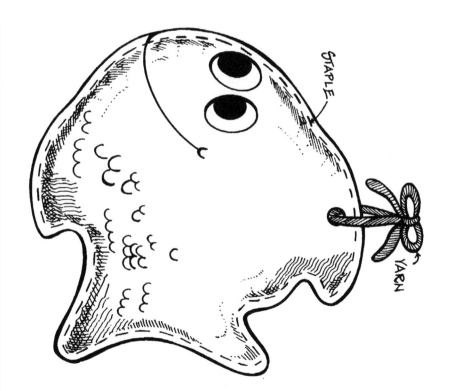

STAPLE

YARN

CAUTION

Life-Size Animal

Materials

collection of large and medium cardboard boxes, cardboard cylindrical ice cream containers and other cardboard materials

wide masking tape or duct tape

wheat paste in large tub or bucket

newspaper, torn in half sheets

fabric scraps, sewing scraps or colored paper

tempera paints and paintbrushes

Art Process

1. Assemble and practice "building" a cardboard animal with boxes. Do not glue, tape or otherwise secure the shape. Form the sculpture first.

2. When satisfied with the size and configuration, use wide masking tape or duct tape to hold the animal together.

3. Dip and soak a half sheet of newspaper briefly in the bucket of wheat paste until wet and coated. Squeeze out the excess paste.

4. With bare hands, press the sheet of newspaper over the animal shape. Press out the wrinkles with bare hands or use a damp small towel.

5. Add layers of newspaper over the box animal until completely covered. Some extra bumps, curves and features can be added with balls, lumps and mounds of soaked paper if desired.

6. Dry the sculpture several days until crunchy and hollow sounding.

7. Paint the box animal with tempera or decorate with fabrics and papers.

HINT · Artists love to build something really large. The mess of working with wheat paste and newspaper is compensated by the creativity and joy of sculpting something life-sized.

· Keep a bucket of soapy water handy for washing hands

CONSTRUCTION

Wood Bas-Relief

Materials

wood scraps
piece of masonite or thin plywood for background
white glue
newspapers
paints and brushes, optional

Art Process

1. Place a piece of masonite or thin plywood on the floor. (Protect the floor with newspaper if needed.)
2. Using small puddles of glue, lay wood scraps flat against the masonite (as opposed to standing straight like a building or sculpture).
3. Dry the project overnight.
4. When dry, the bas-relief can be painted with one or several colors.

Variations

• Thick yarn can be glued into the relief between the scraps.
• With thinned glue add magazine pictures, wrapping paper or other paper to entirely coat and cover the pieces of wood. The artist may also choose to add more pieces of wood.
• Build a stand-up sculpture. Masking tape can help hold the sculpture while glue dries.

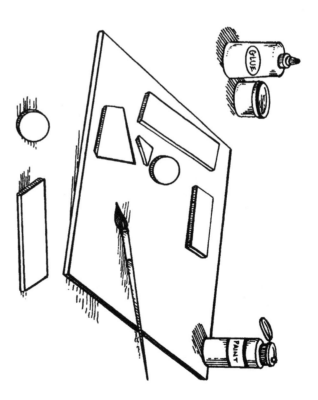

HINT

• Good sources for wood scraps include framing shops, high school shop classes, cabinet shops and construction sites.
• A glue gun can be used for rapid construction and sculpting with one-on-one adult supervision.

CONSTRUCTION

Nail Collage

Materials

nails of all lengths and sizes, with heads and without

hammer

square of thick plywood

wood shop or craft table

decorative items such as yarn, beads, ribbons or rubber bands

pencil

Art Process

1. Draw a simple design or object on the plywood with the pencil.
2. Nail one kind of nail into the penciled design. Try to keep all of one kind of nail the same height.
3. Now use another type of nail on a different part of the design, keeping those about the same height.
4. Proceed with other types of nails.
5. If desired, add decorations to the design by securing them among the nails.

Variations

- Make a board with nails and use rubber bands for the designs.
- String embroidery floss from nail to nail for a spider web effect.
- Before nailing, cover the board with glued magazine pictures, paint, wrapping paper or art tissue.

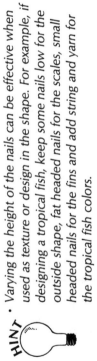

HINT
- Varying the height of the nails can be effective when used as texture or design in the shape. For example, if designing a tropical fish, keep some nails low for the outside shape, fat headed nails for the scales, small headed nails for the fins and add string and yarn for the tropical fish colors.

- Random designs are commonly the choice of young artists rather than realistic shapes like fish.

CONSTRUCTION

Cardboard Stabile

Materials

corrugated cardboard
paper cutter, if possible
scissors
white glue in bottle
covered work area
paint and brushes, optional
masking tape, optional

Art Process

1. **Adult** cuts geometric shapes such as triangles, rectangles and squares from corrugated cardboard about three to five inches each in size. Use a paper cutter to save time and sore fingers.
2. Cut a small notch or slit in one of the sides of each piece.
3. Push the two pieces together, notch to notch.
4. Add a drop of glue to make the two pieces stay together.
5. Join on another pair of cardboard shapes in this way. Continue joining pairs of cardboard shapes. You may use a piece of masking tape to hold the cardboard and remove later or leave on.
6. Completely dry overnight or for two days.
7. Now join pairs with other pairs, cutting and gluing the notches as before. Create a small or even a very large sculpture. Dry again.
8. Remove masking tape or leave as is. Paint the sculpture when dry, if desired.

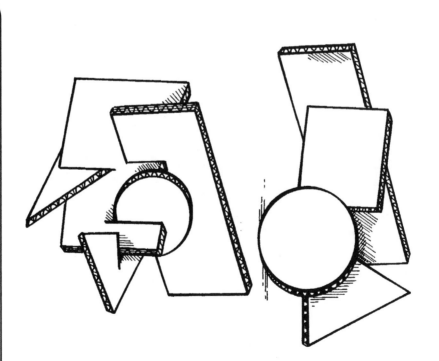

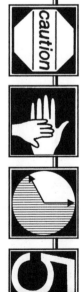

HINT

- Sculptures need balance or they will fall over. Sometimes when a sculpture falls over it becomes a completely new motivation in its new shape for the artist.
- Stabiles are a great group project

CONSTRUCTION

Lace Rubbing

Materials

jumbo crayons, peeled
scraps of lace, fabric or plastic cut into hearts, squares, circles, strips or any shapes
white drawing paper
masking tape, optional

Art Process

1. Select lace shapes and place them on the table. Place a loop of masking tape on the backs of the shapes, if desired, and stick them to the table.
2. Place a sheet of white drawing paper over the shapes. You may tape the corners of the paper to the table to help keep the paper wiggle free.
3. Rub peeled crayons back and forth over the shapes under the paper. A rubbing will emerge.

Variation

- Move shapes around, change colors, try new shapes, make greeting cards or cut out shapes to hang in the window or from the ceiling.

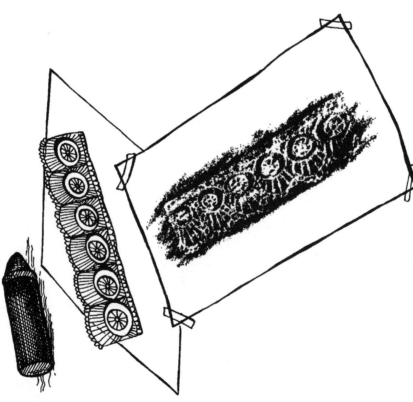

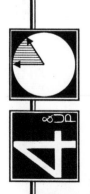

HINT
- Help the artist draw or trace a heart shape.
- Children's rubbings are not always like an adult's. Very young children are just learning the idea of rubbings and to control the crayon. Be patient.

Baked Stubs

Materials

old crayon stubs, peeled
matte board or cardboard
cookie sheet covered with foil
rocks, shells, felt squares, pieces of wood and other items
hot sunny day or 250 degree oven
craft sticks or coffee stir sticks

Art Process

1. Peel the paper from old broken crayons.
2. Place the matte board or cardboard on the covered cookie sheet.
3. Place peeled crayons on the matte board, randomly or by stacking them.
4. Add rocks or shells in and around the crayons if desired.
5. Leave the arrangement in the hot sun to melt, or an **adult** should place the cookie sheet in a 250 degree oven for about ten minutes.
6. An **adult** should remove the hot sheet from the oven.
7. The artist may wish to push the melted crayon about with the craft sticks before the melted design cools.
8. Cool the design completely. Remove it from the cookie sheet.

Variation

· Melt crayon stubs on felt squares, fabric scraps, thin boards, cardboard or other sturdy papers or materials.

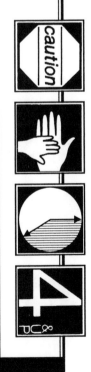

HINT · An adult should do all the "hot" steps such as placing the tray in the oven and removing it from the oven. For safety reasons, be sure the tray is reasonably cool before the child pokes at the melted crayons.

DRAWING

Chalk Rub

Materials

scrap paper
colored chalk
construction paper, light colors
facial tissues

Art Process

1. Tear scrap paper into any pieces or shapes.
2. Rub chalk on the edges of the paper shapes.
3. Place the chalked shapes on light colored construction paper and hold with the non-drawing hand.
4. Brush the chalk from the edge of the torn paper and out onto the construction paper with the facial tissue. This creates a stencil with blurred edges.

Variation

• See page 158, Three Heart Stencils, for a different technique.

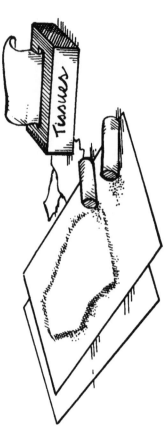

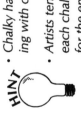

HINT · Chalky hands and fingers are a natural result of creating with chalk.
· Artists tend to want to use a new piece of tissue for each chalk rub shape but encourage using one piece for the entire creation.

D R A W I N G

Crayon-Chalk Transfer

Materials
colored chalk (soft variety called pastels)
2 crayons (one white, one any other color)
square of matte board or cardboard (5" x 5" – 13 cm x 13 cm –)
sheet of smooth paper
masking tape, optional
blunt pencil or paintbrush handle

Art Process
1. Apply chalk colors heavily to the matte board or cardboard. Tap the board to remove dust. Cover the whole board or just certain parts.
2. Color with the white crayon over the chalk colors. This step takes lots of muscles and determination.
3. Coat the white crayon with any other color crayon. Again this needs even more muscles and determination.
4. Place the sheet of smooth paper on top of the colored matte board. Tape down to hold with masking tape.
5. Draw on the smooth paper with a blunt pencil or a paintbrush handle (press firmly). The chalk and crayon colors will transfer from the matte board to the smooth paper.

Variations
· Experiment with textures of matte board, colors of paper and types of chalk.
· Do this project on patterned paper or a watercolor painting which has dried.

HINT
· Chalk breaks and blurs easily. This is the natural condition of chalk and is nothing to worry about.
· Motivated, energetic artists enjoy the challenge of all the coloring and covering. Some young artists tire easily or may not be as artistically driven to complete this project.

Three Heart Stencils

Materials

old file folders
paper towels or tissues
colored chalk
scissors

crayons
construction paper
felt pens

Art Process

Cut heart shapes (or any shapes) from the old file folders using scissors. Shapes can be drawn first or cut freehand. Keep both the shape and the hole left in the folder from the cut shape.

#1 Chalk Stencil

1. Place a shape cut from a file folder (or the hole left in the file folder) on a sheet of paper. White works well. Use the chalk to draw around or inside the shape.
2. While still holding the shape in place, brush the chalk marks with a tissue or paper towel, blurring the lines and softening the color. Now remove the shape and see the designs left behind.

#2 Felt Pen Fingers

1. Place the hole made from a cut stencil on a sheet of paper. Color one finger tip with felt pen until the pad of the finger is very bright.
2. Press the colored finger onto the paper which shows through the hole. Let the print overlap onto the stencil around the hole. Fill the entire shape with fingerprints. Remove the stencil and look at the design left behind.

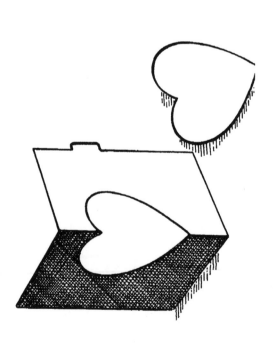

#3 Crayon Stencil Pattern

1. Place a stencil cut from the old file folder on a sheet of paper (or use the hole). Trace around it with crayon.
2. Now move the stencil slightly, overlapping the stencil on the design just traced. Trace the new location of the stencil. Use any colors. Keep moving the stencil and tracing it until the designs look like they have moved across the paper or in a pattern.

HINT · Young artists often need help drawing and cutting hearts. Sometimes it helps to have a shape to trace, or simply let the child design a shape. Most artists want a heart; in this case, help may be needed to make the heart shapes only.

Tissue Stain

Materials

colored tissue paper, 3 or 4 colors torn into small pieces
matte board or cardboard
paintbrushes
water in cups
spray bottles filled with water
covered table

Art Process

1. Place torn bits of colored tissue paper on the matte board or cardboard. Several colors or just one color can be used.
2. Spray water on the tissue pieces. Use a wet paintbrush to enhance the staining from the tissues.
3. Remove or peel away the wet tissue pieces and a stained design will be left behind.
4. Dry the project completely.
5. Add more colors after the design has dried if desired.

Variations

- Do this project on hard boiled eggs, white fabric, paper towels, coffee filters, napkins or white tissue paper.
- Cut the base in a holiday or theme shape, such as a heart for Valentine's Day.

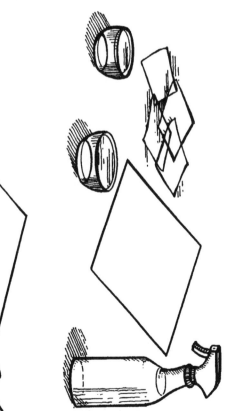

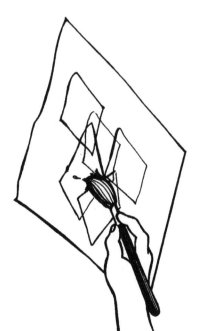

HINT

- Fingers become stained too, so have a bucket of soapy warm water and a towel handy. Sometimes it takes several days for the stain to wear away.

PAINTING

Tissue Color Paint

Materials
art tissues in many colors
paintbrushes
cups of water
paper (white works well)

Art Process
1. Tear or cut tissue into small pieces and shapes.
2. Place the tissue pieces in the cups of water and stir with paintbrushes.
3. When the water is colored, paint with the colored water on paper.

Variation
· Using liquid starch, attach tissue pieces to white paper. Dip a paintbrush into clear water and paint over the tissue pieces so that the color spreads out onto the paper.

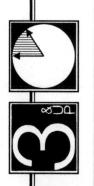

HINT · Use pet food dishes with straight sides for containers of water that will not tip over or spill.

P A I N T I N G

Foil Painting

Materials

aluminum foil
matte board or cardboard
tape (optional)
1/2 cup (115 ml) thick tempera paint in a cup
1 teaspoon dishwashing liquid
paintbrushes

Art Process

1. Cover a piece of matte board or cardboard with aluminum foil, folding the foil around the back of the board.
2. Tape the foil if desired.
3. Add one teaspoon of dishwashing liquid to the thick tempera paint.
4. Paint on the foil. Let the project dry.

Variation

· Cover a box, bottle, or picture frame with foil. Paint as above.

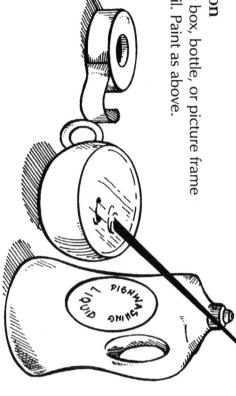

BACK SIDE

HINT · The dishwashing liquid helps the paint adhere to foil, plastic or other glossy surfaces. If it isn't sticking, add another one-half teaspoon dishwashing liquid to the paint.

P
A
I
N
T
I
N
G

3

Sprinkle Paint

Materials

heavy paper taped to table with masking tape
brushes
water
watercolor paints
rubbing alcohol
eyedroppers
rock salt or table salt

Art Process

1. Brush water all over the heavy paper until covered.
2. Paint with watercolors on the wet paper.
3. **Adult** helps drip rubbing alcohol from the eyedropper on the paper and then sprinkle the painting with salt. Closely supervise this step.
4. Dry the artwork completely.
5. Brush off the salt when dry.
6. Carefully remove the tape and lift the paper from the table.

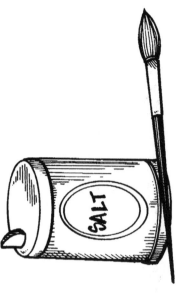

HINT
· The alcohol and salt cause an unusual artistic effect. However, the alcohol can be omitted in step 3, still sprinkling the work with salt
· Use big brushes that hold lots of water to wet paper.
· Dry the painting in place rather than removing to another area.

PAINTING

Stamp a Doodle

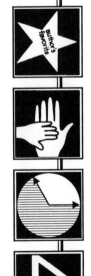

Materials

styrofoam cup
play clay or plasticine
variety of printing materials such as beads, corks, small tiles,
    buttons or other small objects
plaster of Paris mixed to a creamy consistency
tempera paint
paper towel in styrofoam tray
paintbrush or spoon for spreading paint
paper

Art Process

1. Cut the cup in half. Use the bottom half of the cup.
2. Press some clay into the bottom of the cup.
3. Push various little items into the clay.
4. **Adult** pours plaster of Paris into the cup until it is about one
   inch (2.5 cm) deep.
5. When the plaster has hardened and dried, take it out of the cup.
   Also remove the clay.
6. The plaster section is the stamp.
7. Pour some paint on the paper towel in the styrofoam tray.
8. Spread the paint with a brush or a spoon.
9. Press the stamp into the paint and then press it on a piece of
   paper to make a self-created stamp print.

Variation

· Use the stamp prints to make wrapping paper, greeting cards,
  wall paper or stationery.

HINT

· Plaster hardens quickly so have everything ready to
  go when it's time to pour the plaster.
· Although fairly involved, this project makes very
  interesting stamps and is worth the time and trouble.

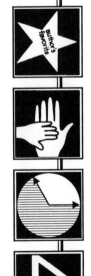

Candy Clay

Materials

1/3 cup (70 g) of butter or margarine
1/3 cup (75 ml) light corn syrup
1/2 teaspoon of salt
1 teaspoon of vanilla
1 lb (450 g) box of powdered sugar
bowl

measuring cups and spoons
clean work surface
spatula or knife
food coloring
paper towels
plain graham crackers

Art Process

1. Wash hands and work surface.
2. Mix the first four ingredients in a bowl with the hands.
3. Mix in the powdered sugar. Knead the dough until smooth.
4. Add more powdered sugar if necessary to make the clay non-sticky and pliable.
5. Divide the clay into small portions and mix in food colors or paste food dye. Use a spatula or spreading knife to mix the colors.
6. Work with bits of the colored candy clay on a paper towel and decorate a plain graham cracker.
7. Eat your creation!

Variation

- Prepare a butter cream frosting and decorate a cake, cupcakes or graham crackers and then place the candy clay designs on this frosting background.

HINT · There should be enough clay from this batch for a group of thirty to decorate one graham cracker or cupcake or for one artist to decorate thirty crackers or cupcakes.

· Do not make candy clay on a hot day or the butter will melt and make the clay too sticky.

· Upright sculptures such as standing animals or people won't work; flat figures and designs work best.

D O U G H

Apple Heart Pizza

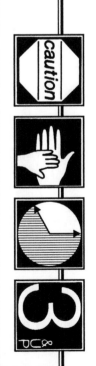

Materials

2-1/4 cups (450 g) flour
1-1/4 sticks butter, room temperature
3 tablespoons, and 1 teaspoon sugar
1/4 teaspoon salt
1/4 cup cold water
3 medium-sized apples
1/2 teaspoon cinnamon
oven at 400 degrees

spatula
cookie sheet
cutting board
hot pads
large mixing bowl
medium mixing bowl
rolling pin
apple peeler/corer

Art Process

The dough:

1. In a large mixing bowl, mix the flour and butter with fingers until the flour looks a little yellow.
2. Add three tablespoons of sugar and the salt to the flour, blending with the hands.
3. Add the cold water and continue to blend with the hands until the dough forms a ball.
4. Spread a little flour on a cutting board. Knead the dough on the floured board for five minutes. Add more flour if needed.
5. Shape the dough into a ball. Divide the ball into four equal pieces. Roll each piece with the rolling pin about one-quarter inch thick. Sprinkle flour on the dough to keep it from sticking.
6. Shape each piece into a flat heart shape by hand. Slide a spatula under the dough and place it on the cookie sheet. Do the same for the other three pieces.

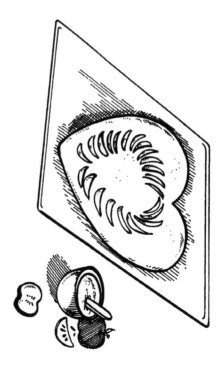

The apple pizza:

1. Core and peel the apples. Cut them in four quarters and then slice each quarter into about six to ten slices.
2. Place all the slices in a medium bowl. Sprinkle with one teaspoon of sugar and the cinnamon. Toss the apples, cinnamon and sugar until evenly coated.
3. Place the apple slices on each heart of dough in a pinwheel shape or any other design.
4. Bake for fifteen minutes at 400 degrees. When the edge is golden brown, the apple pizza hearts are ready. **Adult** removes the pizza from the oven.
5. Slide each pizza onto a plate. Eat hot, warm or cool.

HINT · The dough can be rolled out ahead of time and kept covered in the refrigerator until ready to add the apples and bake.

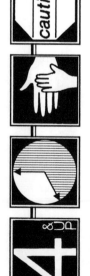

Stained Glass Cookies

Materials

1/3 cup (70 g) vegetable shortening
1/3 cup (70 g) sugar
1 egg
3 cups (600 g) flour with 1/2 teaspoon baking soda added
1 teaspoon salt, scant (optional)
2/3 cup (150 ml) honey
bowl
measuring cups, spoons
crushed lollipops or hard candies
aluminum foil covered cookie sheet
oven at 375 degrees

Art Process

1. Wash hands before beginning. Mix the first five ingredients to make the cookie dough with your hand in a bowl.

2. Roll the dough into snake shapes about one-quarter inch fat for the outlines of the cookies.

3. Use the dough to make cookie designs on aluminum foil on a cookie sheet. Make any free-form designs, hearts, circles, cars, birds, faces or other ideas. Be sure to connect ends of the dough rolls like the outline of a picture.

4. Sprinkle the colored crushed candy into the spaces of the cookies, filling the spaces completely and heaping slightly.

5. Bake the cookies at 375 degrees for eight to ten minutes.

6. **Adult** removes the cookies from the oven to cool. When dough is cool and firm, gently peel off the aluminum foil from the stained glass cookie. Delicious when cool!

HINT · If adding sticks, be sure the oven is big enough or cookies are small enough to fit in the oven once the stick is added.

· Experiment with colors of crushed candy, although red always seems to be a favorite.

DOUGH

Tissue Contact

Materials

clear contact paper
art tissue, variety of colors
scissors
hole punch
yarn
optional collage items such as bits of lace, thread, confetti, glitter or hole punches

Art Process

1. Cut a rectangle of clear contact paper about six by twelve inches (15 cm x 30 cm) or any other size.
2. Fold the rectangle in half. Peel the backing half way off the back, stopping at the fold.
3. Lay the clear side of the clear contact paper on the table, sticky side up.
4. Using any little torn or cut pieces of art tissue, attach them to the sticky contact paper. No glue is necessary. Holiday shapes such as hearts or flowers can also be used.
5. When a design is complete, pull the remainder of the contact paper backing off.
6. Fold over the remaining contact paper and stick it to the design.
7. Take scissors and trim the ragged edges.
8. If desired, punch a hole in the top of the design, add a piece of yarn and hang the artwork in a window or near a light source.

Variation

· Cut the finished contact paper design into a heart shape for a pretty Valentine.

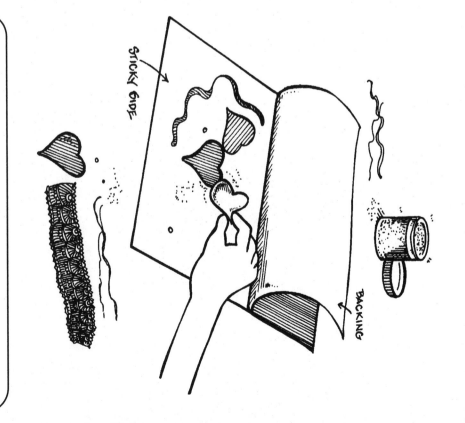

HINT · The folding steps can be very wrinkly and off center depending on the ages and abilities of the artists. Accept this outcome.

C
O
L
A
G
E

Heart a L'Art

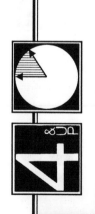

Materials

variety of papers—wrapping paper, magazine pictures, colored paper, tissue paper, posters or book jackets

scissors

glue

matte board or cardboard

crayons, felt pens, paints or any drawing/coloring tools

heart-shaped stencils or patterns

Art Process

1. Trace heart-shaped patterns or stencils on any variety of papers or draw hearts free hand.
2. Cut out the shapes. Use the heart-shaped holes left from the hearts too.
3. Begin gluing hearts on the matte board or cardboard in any design or pattern desired.
4. Add drawings with pen or crayon on the matte board too, if desired.
5. Some artists like to fill the entire matte board with hearts, while other prefer a simple approach.

Variation

- Use the hearts for Valentine cards, mobiles, posters or wall decorations.

HINT
- Hearts are often difficult to draw but are so enjoyed by young children that stencils and patterns are fun to use once in awhile.

Heart Flutters

Materials

one sheet of wax paper, folded and opened
white glue in a dish, thinned with water until milky
   (add a few drops of liquid detergent to prevent beading)
big paintbrush
art tissue
scissors
newspaper covered table
hole punch
yarn or rubber bands

Art Process

1. Brush thinned white glue on half of the wax paper.
2. Stick heart shapes or pieces and patterns of torn or cut art tissue in any colors all over the sticky wax paper. Valentine colors would be effective for a fluttery decoration.
3. Brush more white glue over the hearts or tissue designs.
4. Fold the rest of the wax paper over the design.
5. Dry overnight.
6. Cut the dry tissue collage into long skinny shapes or strips—snakes, lightning or other shapes.
7. Punch a hole in the top of each strip.
8. Loop a rubber band or piece of yarn through the hole.
9. Hang the heart flutters from a stick, a hanger or from pins in the frames around a window.

Variations

• Make bookmarks instead of flutters.
• Frame the tissue collage instead of cutting it into strips.

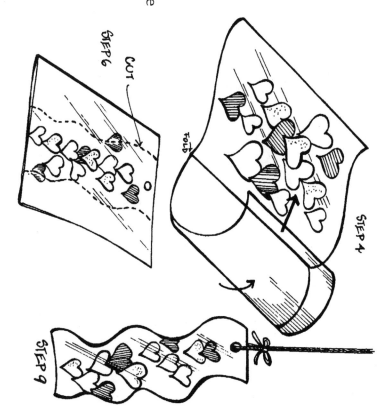

 HINT
• Punch the hole at least one-third inch from the end to prevent tearing.
• Expect the wet glue to look cloudy; it will dry clear.

C
O
L
L
A
G
E

Sewing Cards

Materials

tag board or old file folders
heavy cord, yarn or colored string in pre-cut lengths
paper punch
scissors
masking tape
crayons or felt pens

Art Process

1. Cut the tag board or old file folders into six by six inch (15 cm x 15 cm) squares or any other shapes.
2. Use the paper punch to make holes around the edges of the tag board shape.
3. Tape the end of the yarn with masking tape to make a darning needle-like point.
4. Tape the other end of the yarn to the back of the tag board. Begin sewing the yarn through the holes and making any shapes, designs or patterns desired.
5. When the yarn runs out, tape the end to the back of the board and continue with a new piece or new color.
6. When the sewing is complete, color in between where the yarns cross over making triangles, squares and other shapes. Use crayon, felt pen or both.

Variations

· Complete this project on styrofoam grocery trays or paper plates shaped in designs such as hearts, flowers, cars or cats.
· Have pre-punched materials for the artists to sew.
· Use heart-shaped materials for Valentine's Sewing Cards.

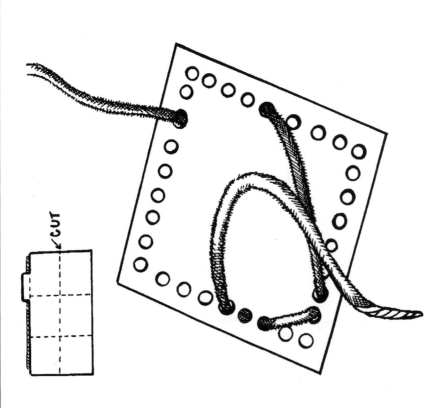

CUT

HINT · If punching the holes is too difficult for the artist, an adult can take directions and punch the holes as the artist directs.
· A heavy duty hole punch is sharper and cuts through thicker paper with ease.

CRAFT

Easy Tubescope

Materials

cardboard tube, any diameter from small to large
wax paper
art tissue scraps
hole punch
scissors
white glue thinned with water
paintbrush
tape or heavy rubber band

Art Process

1. Cut a piece of wax paper into a circle one to two inches larger than the end of the cardboard tube.
2. Using the paintbrush dipped in thinned glue, brush bits of art tissue on the wax paper circle. Pieces can be torn, cut with scissors, or little circles made with a hole punch can be used.
3. Dry the wax paper, glue and tissue overnight.
4. When dry, place the wax paper design over the end of the cardboard tube and press the edges over the edges of the tube. Tape the wax paper circle to the tube or use a heavy rubber band.
5. Look through the other end of the tube to see the colors and designs. Hold the colors up to the light too.

Variations

· Use plastic wrap or cellophane instead of wax paper.
· Cover the other open end of the tube with cellophane.

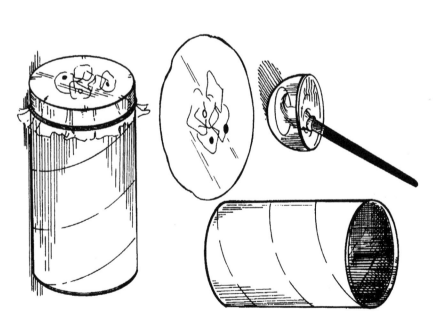

HINT · Young artists often like to look through colored cellophane, tissues and papers before sticking them to the wax paper so they can decide which colors are most effective for them to use on their own Tubescope.

C
R
A
F
T

String Snacks

Materials
embroidery floss or crochet thread
scissors
large-eyed plastic needle
food items—dry cereal with holes, raisins, prunes, dried apricots
   or gum drops
beads made from baked bread dough

Art Process
1. Thread floss through the needle. Knot the doubled thread at one end.
2. String various food items on the thread until the string is full.
3. Cut the end of the string at the needle and tie this end to the other end of the string making a complete circle, necklace or garland of food.
4. Wear, eat and enjoy! A real portable snack!

Variations
- String a small box of raisins to the necklace as a pendant.
- Fill squares of plastic wrap with seeds or nuts and attach these to the necklace too.
- Use patterns in the design such as dark/light, smooth/rough or large/small.
- Go for a walk while wearing snack-necklaces.
- Make the necklaces for gifts.

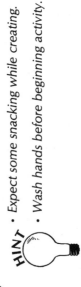

HINT
- Expect some snacking while creating.
- Wash hands before beginning activity.

C
R
A
F
T

Colorful Stir Sticks

Materials
wooden coffee stir sticks
powdered dye or food coloring
warm water in baking pan
paper towels, newspaper
masking tape
tongs or wide spatula

Art Process
1. Mix powdered dye or food coloring in the warm water in the baking pan. Make several pans of different colors, if desired.
2. Place wooden stir sticks in the warm dye.
3. Remove the sticks with the tongs or a spatula and place on the newspaper to dry. Drying takes several hours or overnight.
4. When dry, build a sculpture by taping the stir sticks together with bits of masking tape.

Variation
• For a holiday or Valentine theme, glue little paper hearts or lace to the finished sculpture.

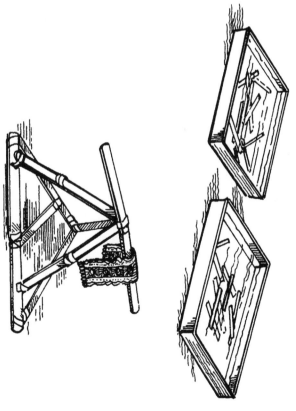

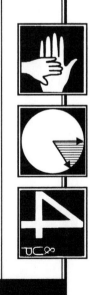

HINT
• A warm dye mixture colors the wood faster than a cool mixture.
• The dye also colors hands and fingers, so wear rubber gloves or use tongs to lift the wet sticks out of the dye.
• Dye match sticks, craft sticks or other wooden items to use for sculpture.

King Size Rope Wrap

Materials

rope, yarn, string or cord
square of plywood at least 1/2" (1.5 cm) thick and 2' (70 cm) square (or larger)
hammer
nails with large heads, 1/2" (1.5 cm) or less in length
optional—feathers, cotton balls, ribbon or other decorative odds and ends

Art Process

1. Hammer nails into the plywood square in any design. Nails can go around the edge, or may be hammered into the center. An **adult** should carefully supervise this step and watch to see that nails do not go all the way through the plywood and into the floor or table.
2. When there are sufficient nails, take rope or yarn and begin winding, wrapping, tying and weaving around the various nails to form colorful designs.
3. Add optional decorations to the yarn or rope as desired.

Variations

- Make this a group project with an even larger sheet of plywood, more nails and more artists working together.
- Paint the wood background first.
- Cover the wood with wrapping paper or contact paper first.

HINT · Some artists need help tying the yarns and rope around the nails. Masking tape can also help.

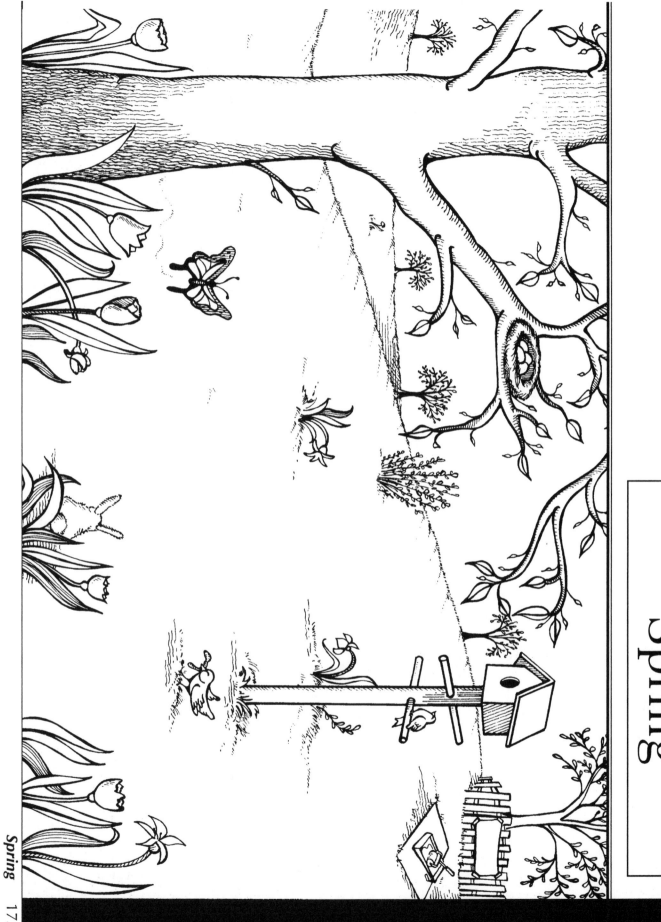

Tape and Chalk Stencil

Materials

masking tape
matte board or cardboard
damp sponge
colored chalk

Art Process

1. Apply masking tape to the matte board or cardboard in any design.
2. Rub chalk on a damp sponge or draw designs on a damp sponge.
3. Press the chalked sponge all over the taped matte board or cardboard. The chalk will stick to the paper.
4. Peel off the masking tape and a stencil design from the tape will be left.

Variations

- This same project can be done with masking tape and watercolor paint. Paint the paper or matte board with watercolor paints instead of the chalk. Peel off the tape and a negative design will be left.
- Cut the masking tape in shapes.
- Use clear contact paper instead of masking tape.

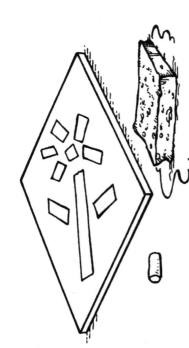

HINT · Do not leave tape on the paper too long or it will not come off.
· Leave a little edge of tape sticking up and it will be easier to peel off.

DRAWING

Sandpaper Melt

Materials

electric warming tray covered in foil
peeled crayons
sandpaper, medium grade
thick work gloves to protect hands

Art Process

1. Place the sandpaper on the heated warming tray.
2. Wear a thick work glove on the non-drawing hand to protect
   against burns while holding the sandpaper down.
3. Slowly draw or rub the peeled crayon over the heated sandpaper.
4. Remove the sandpaper from the warming tray when the design
   is complete. The drawing will cool and harden.

Variation

· Draw on typing paper, drawing paper or experiment with other
  papers on the warming tray.

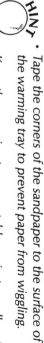

HINT
· Tape the corners of the sandpaper to the surface of
  the warming tray to prevent paper from wiggling.
· Keep the warming tray on a table against a wall and
  tape the cord to the table to prevent tripping over
  cord.
· Observe caution with the warming tray. One-on-one supervision is necessary for projects involving heat.

Fabric Starched Chalk

Materials
square of cotton fabric
liquid starch in a bucket or bowl
tray
water
colored chalk

Art Process
1. Soak cotton fabric in the bowl of liquid starch.
2. Wring out the fabric with your hands.
3. Place the fabric on a tray and smooth out the wrinkles.
4. Use colored chalk to draw on the wet fabric.
5. Dry the artwork in place or remove to another drying area and dry flat.

Variations
- Work with a textured surface under the fabric so chalk will pick up the design of the texture underneath the fabric.
- Frame the completed design or display in an embroidery hoop.

HINT
- The chalk will be brighter when moistened by the starch. It will stay on the fabric better than a dry fabric and chalk art project.
- Do not wash this fabric or the design will wash out

D
R
A
W
I
N
G

Layered Color-Muffins

Materials

old crayons, peeled and separated by color

griddle covered with aluminum foil

metal cup or small pan (lined with foil), a muffin tin,
  metal ice cube tray, or candy mold

oven mitts

Art Process

1. Place one color of crayon pieces in a metal cup on the hot
   griddle.
2. Melt the crayon until liquid.
3. Pour a thin layer of melted crayon into a mold. Cool completely.
4. Melt another color of crayon.
5. Pour a thin layer of the second color on top of the first color.
   Cool completely.
6. Continue to layer colors of melted crayon until mold is full.
   Cool completely.
7. When completely cool, pop the layered crayon muffin out of
   the mold and use to color on paper.

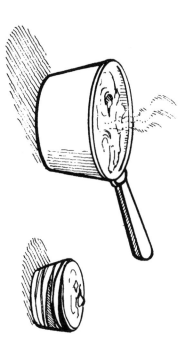

HINT

- Cool the crayon layers in the freezer for quick results.
- Observe caution in all steps involving the heated griddle. This project requires one-on-one supervision with an adult to prevent injury or burns.

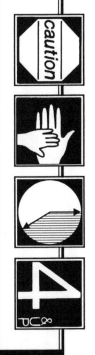

caution

DRAWING

4

Sandpaper Print

Materials

sandpaper, medium grade
crayons
newspaper
old iron, very warm
white paper

Art Process

1. Draw on the sandpaper with crayons, pressing hard.
2. Place a thick pad of newspaper on a table where the iron is set up to press.
3. Carry sandpaper to ironing area.
4. Cover the sandpaper with a sheet of white paper.
5. **Adult** irons the white paper on the sandpaper, allowing the crayon marks to melt onto the white paper.
6. To make several prints of the same crayon design, re-color the design with crayons and press again with the iron on a new sheet of white paper.

PRINT FROM
SANDPAPER DRAWING

STEP 1

STEP 4

WHITE PAPER

STEP 5

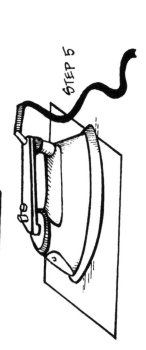

HINT
- This is a great way to produce several copies of prints by one child.
- Some children will be able to do the ironing with supervision. Work at a low table.
- Tape sandpaper to the table so it won't wiggle while the artist is drawing.

D R A W I N G

Glossy Paint

Materials

one can sweetened condensed milk
4 colors food coloring
4 cups
white drawing paper
paintbrushes
cotton swabs
bulletin board
push pins

Art Process

1. Cut shapes from the white drawing paper or draw shapes on the paper.
2. Mix a different color of food coloring with condensed milk in each of the four cups.
3. Use a paintbrush or a cotton swab to paint the shapes in different colors.
4. While the paint is still wet, hang the shapes on a wall with push pins so the paint colors will run together. (A fence or bulletin board works too.)
5. Dry the art for several days.

Variations

- Use this paint idea for painting or designing eggs for Easter or spring themes.
- Mix a combination of bright colors and pastel colors.

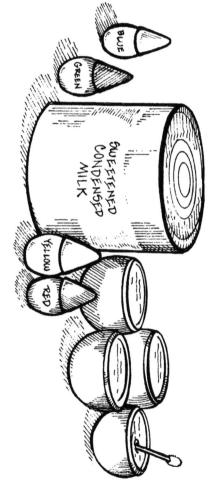

HINT
- You may need to help young children carry the painted shape, push in pins and keep control of the project.
- Cover the floor beneath the dripping paint

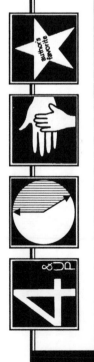

Cornstarch Paint

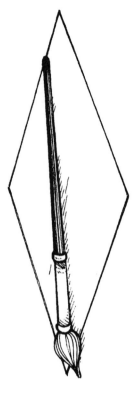

Materials

teaspoon
baby food jar with lid
vinegar
cornstarch
food coloring
paper
paintbrush

Art Process

1. Mix one teaspoon vinegar, one teaspoon cornstarch and twenty drops of food coloring in the baby food jar.
2. Shake the ingredients to mix.
3. Make several different colors in separate jars.
4. Dip a paintbrush into the cornstarch paint and paint on paper as with tempera paint.

Variations

· Paint on hard boiled eggs.
· Paint on wood scraps.
· Experiment painting on other surfaces.

1 TEASPOON VINEGAR

1 TEASPOON CORNSTARCH

20 DROPS OF FOOD COLORING

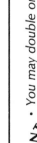

HINT · You may double or triple this recipe if you will need a large supply of this paint.

· Substitute cream or paste food coloring found in cake decorating departments for a brighter paint that goes farther.

· Food coloring can stain clothing, so have soapy water and towels ready. Cover children and table surfaces to prevent spills and stains.

P A I N T I N G

Rolled Egg

Materials

small baking pan
liquid tempera paints, several colors
hard boiled eggs
paper to fit pan
cookie cooling rack
empty egg carton

Art Process

1. Place the paper in the bottom of the baking pan. Trim the paper to fit if necessary.
2. Pour several colors of paint on the paper.
3. Place the egg in the pan.
4. Gently tip the pan and roll the egg through the paints. Tip the pan very slightly and gently or the egg will crash into sides of baking pan.
5. Dry the egg on wire mesh or a cookie cooling rack. The paint can rub off the egg on clothes and hands, especially wet hands, so carry dry eggs in an egg carton.

Variation

- The paper from the bottom of the pan can be an art project, too.

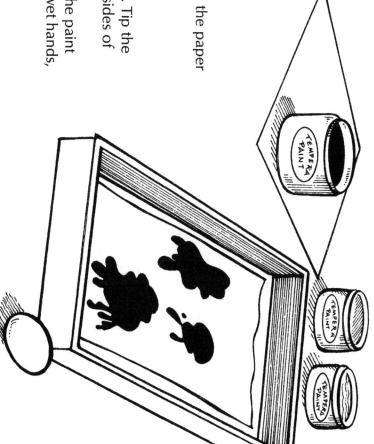

HINT

- Sit down during the tipping stage.
- For very young children, use a small plastic container instead of a baking pan.
- Use food coloring mixed in a half cup of water with one tablespoon of vinegar instead of paint for egg designs that aren't quite as thick as paint.

Batik Eggs

Materials

egg carton or wrinkled aluminum foil for egg drying rack
hard-boiled eggs
crepe paper, several colors
scissors
bowl
hot water
tweezers
1 tablespoon white vinegar
candle, matches
paper towels
covered table

Art Process

1. Cut strips of crepe paper about one-half inch wide. Place them in a bowl. Do the same for additional colors of crepe paper.
2. **Adult** pours hot water on the crepe paper to release the dye. Remove the paper with tweezers or fingers.
3. Add a tablespoon of white vinegar to set the dye. Let cool.
4. **Adult** drips candle wax onto any area of the egg to leave the surface of the egg its natural color.
5. Eggs will be decorated with several applications of wax and dye. Start by dipping the egg in the lightest color of dye first. Dry the egg with a paper towel.
6. **Adult** drips more candle wax onto the parts of the egg the artist wishes to keep a light color of dye. Dip the egg into the next darker dye and dry with a paper towel. (It may take a few minutes for the dye to become the desired color.)
7. To remove the wax, an **adult** places the egg on a tray covered with paper towels in a very warm oven. After the wax has melted, (in about two minutes), wipe the egg with another paper towel. Cool in an egg carton or on wrinkled aluminum foil.

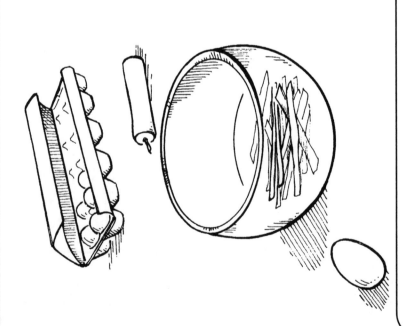

HINT

- This is one of those projects where the adult ends up doing most of the work. Let the child do as much as possible. This is a one-on-one project.

- Fresh eggs can be emptied by poking a pin hole in both ends of the egg and blowing out the contents with a hefty puff of air. The contents can be used for cooking. This leaves a fragile but light, empty egg for dying. This egg will keep indefinitely.

PAINTING

Onion Skin Egg

Materials

uncooked eggs
brown or purple onion skins
squares of old cloth or nylon stockings
small leaves or rice
rubber bands
pot for boiling eggs
stove
paper towels
covered table
cooking oil

Art Process

1. Place the cloth or nylon stocking square on the table.
2. Put about six layers of onion skin on the cloth.
3. Place leaves or bits of rice on top of the onion skins.
4. Place the egg on top of the skins, leaves and rice. Place more onion skins on top of this.
5. Wrap the cloth or nylon stocking around the egg and skins firmly. Wrap several rubber bands around the cloth to keep it in place and to press the onion skins firmly against the egg's surface.
6. **Adult** lowers the wrapped egg into a pot of boiling water for about 30 minutes.
7. Remove the egg from the pot and cool.
8. Remove the cloth and materials from the egg.
9. Rub the egg with a little cooking oil to give it a shine.

HINT • Young children usually need help wrapping the egg firmly in the nylon stocking.

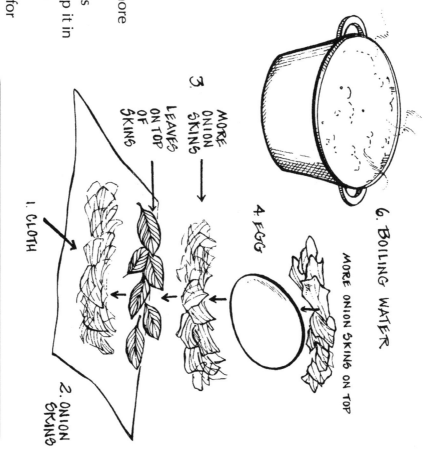

3. MORE ONION SKINS

LEAVES ON TOP OF SKINS

1. CLOTH

4. EGG

2. ONION SKINS

6. BOILING WATER

MORE ONION SKINS ON TOP

caution

P A I N T I N G

Plaster Bag Art

Materials

plaster of Paris

water

plastic sandwich bag

powdered tempera paints

liquid tempera paints, optional

paintbrushes, optional

wooden block or piece of matte board for a base, optional

Art Process

1. Scoop some plaster of Paris into a plastic sandwich bag.
2. Add a tablespoon or more of powdered tempera paint to the plaster.
3. Add some water to form a soft dough.
4. Squeeze the plastic bag with the hands to mix the water, paint and plaster. When the plaster feels warm to the touch, it is beginning to set and will set quickly.
5. Hold the bag in any desired shape as the plaster hardens.
6. When the sculpture is hard, remove it from the bag.
7. Paint further with liquid tempera paint, if desired.
8. Glue the sculpture to a wooden block or piece of matte board for a base, if desired.

HINT · Experiment with the measurements of plaster and water before trying this with young artists. Measurements can vary from day to day, but a half bag of plaster and a quarter cup of water is a good start.

SCULPTURE

Frozen Balloons

Materials

balloons, all shapes and sizes
water
cookie sheet
freezer
large tub or water table, filled with water
eyedroppers
food coloring or watercolor paints

Art Process

1. Fill each balloon with water.
2. Place the balloon on a cookie sheet in the freezer for two days.
3. Remove the balloons from the freezer. Tear and pull away the balloon.
4. Place the frozen balloons in a large tub filled with water or in a water table.
5. Drop food coloring or watercolor paints onto the frozen balloons. Push, float and manipulate the balloons into designs and patterns.

Variations

- Drop colored salty water on the frozen balloons and see what happens.
- Fill the balloons with colored water before freezing.
- Water can be frozen in many different containers, bags and molds to add to the floating ice sculpture.
- Fill the balloons with temera paint thinned with water. "Paint" with the frozen balloons on paper.

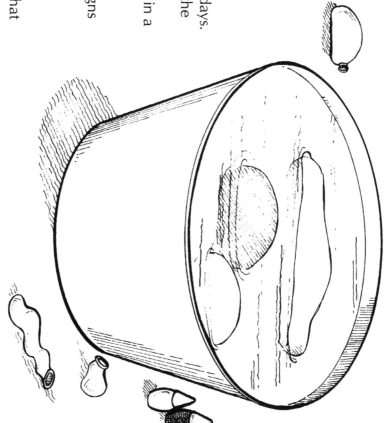

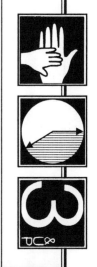

HINT · A group of artists may enjoy standing around the tub of water to watch the colors mix and swirl, the ice balloons float, sink and bump into each other.

Egg Shell Mosaic

Materials

dyed eggs, peeled
wax paper
rolling pin
matte board or cardboard
glue

Art Process

1. Peel dyed eggs such as those used at Easter.
2. Save the shells.
3. Place the shells on wax paper.
4. Crush the shells with a rolling pin.
5. Glue crushed shells on matte board or cardboard.
6. Dry the project.

Variations

- Color on the shells of hard boiled eggs with felt pens instead of dying them. Peel these and use for the colored shells.
- Glue the pieces of egg shell in a definite mosaic pattern on heavy board or paper.
- Use tiny scraps of paper, confetti or paper punch holes in addition to the egg shell.

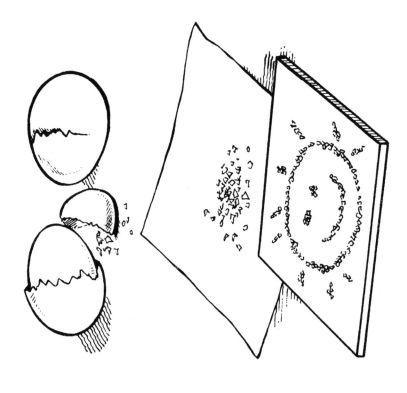

HINT · Young children do not always have the coordination or patience to work with picking up tiny pieces of shell. Give them a toothpick or cotton swab to dip first in glue and then touch to the shell piece. A little dot of glue on the paper will help pull the shell off the toothpick or cotton swab and onto the paper.

C
O
L
L
A
G
E

String Collage

Materials
colorful scraps and pieces of yarn, embroidery floss or string
scissors
liquid starch
heavy paper
styrofoam tray
scissors

Art Process
1. Cut the string or yarn into two foot lengths.
2. Soak the string for a few minutes in a styrofoam tray filled with liquid starch.
3. Place the tray near the edge of the heavy paper.
4. Pull one strand of yarn or string out of the tray.
5. Arrange it on the heavy paper in any shape or design.
6. Repeat with many strands of different colors.
7. Dry the string collage overnight.

Variation
• Add this yarn to a starch-based finger painting and move the yarn around in the painting to form designs.

LIQUID STARCH

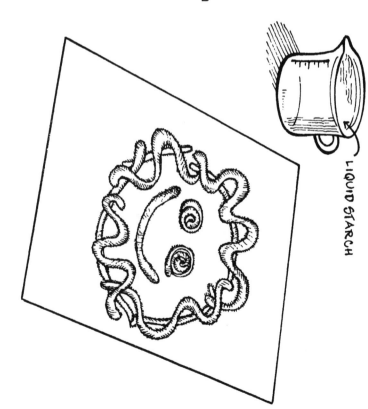

HINT • Glue can be substituted for the starch, and it works just as well.

C
O
L
L
A
G
E

Paper Dolls

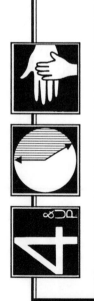

Materials
old file folders
scissors
glue
collage items such as yarn, buttons, beads,
    beans, lace or felt
pens or crayons

Art Process
1. **Adult** helps cut old file folders into the shape of a doll body without features or clothing. The shape should be fairly chubby and thick so it will be strong enough to support gluing.
2. Draw or color on the doll shape before decorating further.
3. Begin decorating the doll shape with collage items for hair, eyes, clothing, jewelry, a hat, glasses or other features to dress the doll.
4. Allow the doll to dry completely.

Variations
- Make characters for a favorite story or play such as the gingerbread boy, a farmer, a farmer's wife and a wolf.
- Make the paper dolls into puppets by taping each one to a dowel or stick so they can be manipulated above a partition or curtain.
- Removable clothing for the doll can be made from paper or fabric scraps.

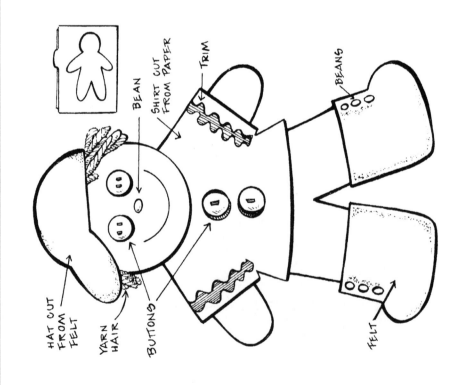

HAT CUT FROM FELT
YARN HAIR
BUTTONS
BEAN
SHIRT CUT FROM PAPER
TRIM
BEANS
FELT

HINT · Young artists tend to use a lot of glue when adding the collage items, so carry the doll flat to a drying area and leave for a day or two. If the doll is carried upright, all the glue and collage items will slide off the doll shape.

COLLAGE

Neon Weave

Materials

black matte board (or cardboard painted black)
  cut in 8" x 8" (20 cm x 20 cm) squares
bright yarns in any lengths (not more than 6' – 2 m –)
tape

Art Process

1. Cut slits one-half inch deep around each side of the square. Young children tend to cut the slits VERY close together like the fringe of a scarf. Encourage them to space the slits about one to two inches apart for a strong weaving. Spaces can be cut much farther apart too. Help as needed.

2. Tape the end of a piece of bright yarn to the back of the square and pull it through one of the slits.

3. Cross the yarn back and forth over the front of the square, pulling it through the slits to hold. Use slits more than once, if needed.

4. When one color of yarn runs out, add new colors of yarn by taping the end of the new color to the back of the square. Continue to wrap, weave, cross and decorate the square.

5. When complete, tape the last end of yarn to the back of the square or simply pull the yarn through one of the slits.

BACK

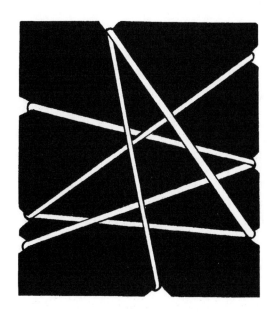

HINT • For easy yarn distribution, roll the yarn into a ball and place in a cardboard box with a lid. Punch a hole in the lid and feed the yarn through the hole. Place the lid back on the box. Now the yarn can be pulled through the lid without tangling. Cut a slit on the edge of the lid. Use this to tuck the loose end of the yarn until the next person will use the yarn. The box can have many balls of yarn and many holes.

C
R
A
F
T

Papier-Mache Bracelets

Materials

cardboard strip about 12" (30 cm) long and
1/2"(1.5 cm) to 2" (5 cm) wide
wallpaper paste
newspaper torn into small strips
about 1/2" x 2" (1.5 cm x 5 cm) strips of thin white paper
clear gloss enamel, optional   liquid starch
stapler   felt pens
tempera paints   scissors
colored tissue paper

Art Process

1. Help the artist measure a cardboard strip bracelet around his or her wrist. Leave enough room to fit the artist's hand loosely and allow for thickness added by the papier-mache.
2. Remove the strip from the wrist, overlap the ends and staple.
3. Dip a piece of newspaper into the wallpaper paste and wrap around the bracelet. Repeat this process until the bracelet is covered with at least three layers of the newspaper.
4. Cover the bracelet with strips of thin white paper so that the newsprint will not show through later. The paper should adhere without extra paste. Add paste if necessary.
5. Dry the bracelets for several days.
6. Decorate the bracelet by painting or drawing. Covering the bracelet with liquid starch and pieces of colored tissue is also pretty.
7. Dry the bracelet again. When dry, an **adult** may paint the bracelet with a clear, glossy paint or polymer to add shine and protect the paint, pen drawings or colored tissue.

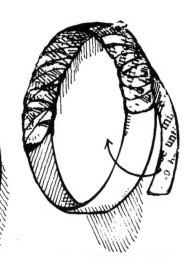

HINT
- One effective way to dry the bracelets is to hang the bracelet over a cardboard tube, clothes hanger or clothesline rope.
- Young artists may need help starting to wrap the papier-mache around the bracelet strip.
- Papier-mache can be a magical wonder to young children. Prepare for being messy and the fun will be worthwhile.

Bonnets

Materials
paper plate
hole punch
string or elastic
decorative items such as ribbon, lace, fabric scraps, beads,
 artificial flowers, bows, felt scraps, streamers, confetti
 or glitter
crayons, felt pens or paints
glue

Art Process
1. An **adult** should punch a hole on each side of the paper plate.
 Tie pieces of string through the holes to make a chin strap to
 hold the bonnet in place when it is complete.
2. Turn the plate upside down on the table.
3. Begin attaching decorations and collage items to the plate to
 create a bonnet. Use crayons or pens to further decorate the
 bonnet.
4. Keep the underside of the hat plain for easier handling. If decorating the underside is desired, have the artist do this before
 decorating the top of the bonnet.
5. Dry the bonnet thoroughly and then wear it.

Variations
• Play music and have the artists march in a bonnet parade.
• Use only tissue scraps, doilies and foil for a daintier design.
• Create a "theme" bonnet, such as the environment, favorites,
 pets.

HINT • Use one piece of elastic attached to both holes of
 the bonnet. Measure the elastic from one side of the
 bonnet, under the child's chin, to the other side of
 the bonnet. No tying necessary!

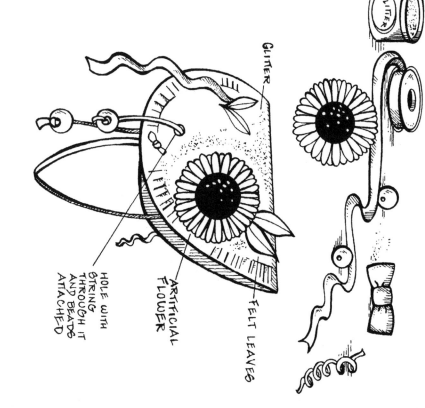

GLITTER

GLITTER

FELT LEAVES

ARTIFICIAL
FLOWER

HOLE WITH
STRING
THROUGH IT
AND BEADS
ATTACHED

Brushed Chalk

Materials

hammer or other crushing tool such as a rock
old ends of colored chalk
small pie tins
liquid starch in cups

paintbrushes
paper

Art Process

1. Place old ends of chalk in pie tins. Gently push the hammer head against the chalk until it crushes. Hold on to the pie tin while crushing. Supervise this activity closely.

2. Place one color of crushed chalk in each pie tin and mix a rainbow of colors together in another pie tin.

3. Using a paintbrush, paint liquid starch on the sheet of paper in any design or pattern.

4. Pinch bits of chalk powder and sprinkle it on the liquid starch design. The chalk will absorb the starch and become bright and moist.

5. If desired, paint over the chalk and starch design with more starch or add more chalk powder. Experiment with the mixing and painting of chalk powder and starch.

6. When complete, dry the project for about an hour.

Variations

- Mix liquid starch in the pie tin with the crushed chalk until the consistency of paste. Paint with the chalk starch mixture on paper.
- Mix the crushed chalk with white glue or sugar water and paint the mixture on paper.

HINT
- *Artists of any age can crush the chalk with some supervision and encouragement. The magic word is "gently." A rock may work better than a hammer for some children. Any crushing tool is fine as long as it works.*

DRAWING

Marking Pen Paint

Materials

water-based marking pens, all colors
absorbent papers such as paper towels, coffee filters,
  blotters or napkins
drawing paper
plastic spray bottle filled with water, nozzle set on spray

Art Process

1. Draw freely with marking pens on a variety of papers.
2. Spray the marking pen designs with water and watch the colors
   blend, blur or separate.

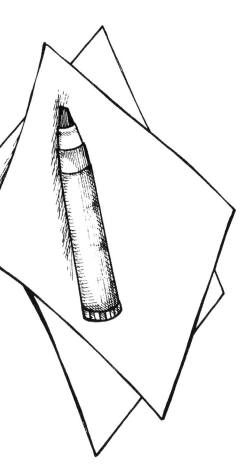

HINT
- Work on a covered surface; wet pen markings can
  soak through onto the table.
- Most pens are water-based but may not say so.
  Permanent pens will not work; these pens are always
  marked "permanent."

D R A W I N G

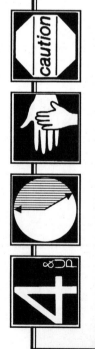

Dig It Crayons

Materials

jumbo crayons

tools such as a plastic knife, toothpick or paper clip

paper

Art Process

1. **Adult** helps the artist cut or dig designs into the sides of the jumbo crayons. Cut wedges, scratch grooves, dig dots and holes or make other shapes. Work on all sides of the crayon. Crayons can break if they are pressed too hard while being carved, but broken pieces can be used for coloring too.

2. Rub and color with the sides of the crayons. Designs will emerge in the picture due to the shapes and designs cut into the crayons.

Variation

· Make a Crayon Rubbing with the grooved crayons. (See p.20)

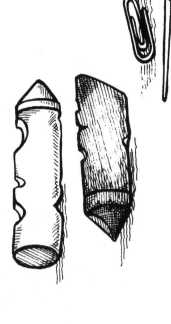

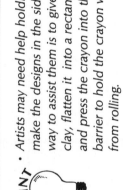

HINT · Artists may need help holding the crayons while they make the designs in the sides of the crayons. One way to assist them is to give the artist a chunk of play clay, flatten it into a rectangle about one inch thick and press the crayon into the clay. This makes a soft barrier to hold the crayon while carving it and keep it from rolling.

D
R
A
W
I
N
G

Towel Chalk Design

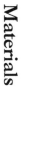
Materials

heavy paper towels
pan of hot water
colored chalk

Art Process

1. Place a heavy paper towel in pan of hot water.
2. Remove the towel, and wring it out. Help is needed.
3. Help the artist place the wet towel on a bare table and smooth out the wrinkles by hand.
4. Draw any design on the wet towel with the colored chalk.

Variations

- Paint on wet paper towels with watercolor paints.
- Drop food coloring or watercolor paints from an eyedropper on the wet towels.

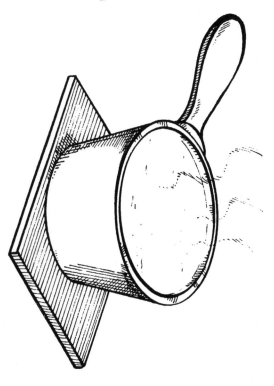

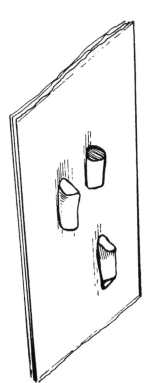

HINT
- Towels tear easily if too much pressure is used with the chalk. Have lots of towels ready as artists experiment with drawing in a way that won't tear the towels. Torn towels are perfectly permissible.

Magic Drawing

Materials

cotton swabs
colored tissue paper
liquid bleach
small bowl
white paper

Art Process

1. **Adult** places about one tablespoon of bleach in a bowl. (Keep the lid on the bleach bottle and keep it out of the reach of children.)
2. Dip the cotton swab into the bleach and draw on the colored tissue paper to make the color fade away.

Variation

· Slip a piece of white paper under the tissue paper so that the design is more clearly visible. Experiment with other colors of paper under the colored tissue paper.

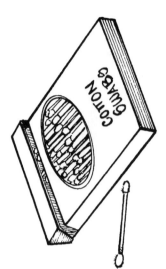

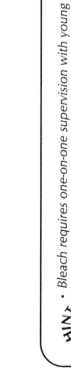

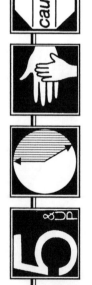

HINT
· Bleach requires one-on-one supervision with young children.
· Remember bleach can take the color out of clothing too, so have children wear aprons or play clothes.

D R A W I N G

Powder Painting

Materials

powdered tempera paint in small pie tins
paintbrushes
liquid starch
paper

Art Process

1. Pour a puddle of liquid starch onto the paper.
2. Spread the starch over the paper with a paintbrush.
3. With a different slightly damp paintbrush, dip into the powdered paint and dab it onto the starch-covered paper.
4. The paint will dissolve and become thicker, creating an unusual texture.

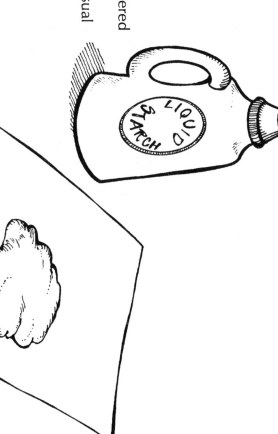

HINT
- Big, heavy paper such as butcher paper works well.
- Pie tins can flip over. You may want to use flat styrofoam grocery trays taped to the table when working with younger children.

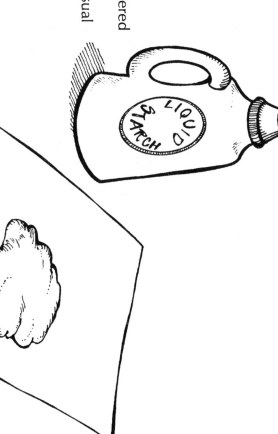

PAINTING

Corn Syrup Color

Materials

matte board or cardboard
food coloring
light corn syrup
paint aprons
craft sticks or spoons

Art Process

1. Pour a small puddle of corn syrup on the matte board or cardboard. Spread it out towards the edges with a craft stick or spoon.
2. Squeeze a few drops of food coloring randomly on the corn syrup.
3. Blend the colors in with the fingers.
4. Dry the artwork for several days for a bright, shiny, rainbow colored design.

Variation

• Use corn syrup colors on an egg-shaped piece of heavy paper for a spring design. You may also choose to make these designs on any shape of paper to complement a theme or holiday.

CORN SYRUP

MATT BOARD

DROPS OF
FOOD COLORING

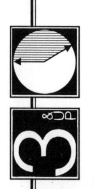

HINT • Clean up is tasty and sticky. Warm water works best.

PAINTING

Egg Paint

Materials

4 egg yolks
4 bowls
food coloring
paper
paintbrush

Art Process

1. With adult help crack eggs and separate egg yolks. Place one egg yolk into each bowl. Save egg whites for other art ideas
2. Add a few drops of food coloring to each yolk and mix. Mix red, blue and yellow food coloring to make a new color in the fourth cup.
3. Paint the bright, glossy colors on the paper.

Variation

· Paint on toast, hot dog buns or sugar cookies. Warm the food or bake briefly to dry the egg paint.

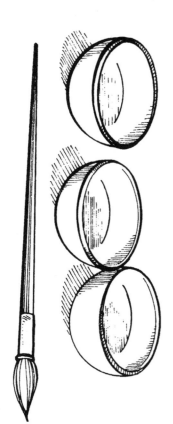

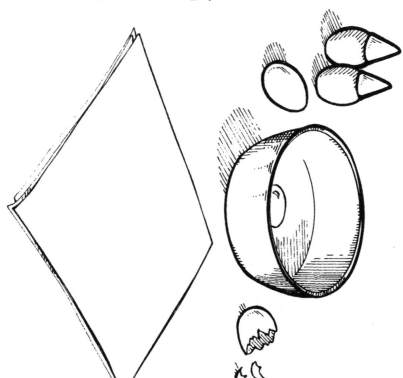

HINT · Use wide bowls which do not tip easily. Styrofoam grocery trays make great containers for mixing the egg yolk and food coloring.
· Add a few drops of water to tray or cup if paint thickens or begins to dry before painting is complete.

P
A
I
N
T
I
N
G

Marbling

Materials

waterproof inks, variety of colors
large styrofoam grocery trays
plastic spoons
light color blotting paper
apron
newspaper covered drying area

Art Process

1. Fill the grocery trays halfway with water.
2. Gently drop a small amount of waterproof ink onto the surface of the water. Add drops of additional colors.
3. Stir the ink over the water with a plastic spoon slowly and carefully. (The ink will swirl and float forming beautiful patterns.)
4. With adult help, place the blotting paper on top of the floating colors for about thirty seconds.
5. With adult help, quickly lift off the paper, turn it over and hold it flat to stop the colors from running.
6. Dry the colored paper on a flat, covered surface. This project can take several days to dry.

Variation

- This project is very pretty to watch using a clear glass bowl with a piece of plain white paper beneath the bowl. Skip the paper printing step and just enjoy watching the colors swirl and mix in the bowl.

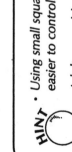

HINT
- Using small squares of paper makes this project easier to control.
- Adult supervision is necessary when working with waterproof ink, both in use and in clean up.

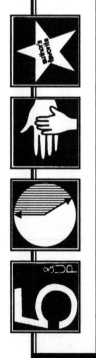

P A I N T I N G

Print Relief

Materials

squares of cardboard or a gift box
scissors
glue
newspapers to cover table
liquid tempera paint in shallow pan
paintbrush
brayer, print roller, child's rolling pin or dowel
paper or cloth

Art Process

1. Draw and cut out a design from the cardboard or gift box.
2. Glue the design to a cardboard backing.
3. Place the cardboard design on the newspaper covered table, design side up.
4. Apply tempera paint over the cardboard design with a paintbrush.
5. Place a piece of fabric or paper over the design.
6. Roll the brayer or rolling pin over the paper or fabric to make a print.
7. Peel the paper or fabric away from the cardboard. The design will transfer to the fabric or paper.
8. Dry the project completely.

Variation

- Brush different colors onto specific parts of the design for a multicolored print.

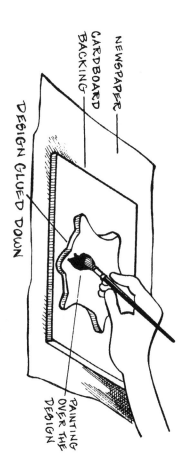

NEWSPAPER
CARDBOARD BACKING
DESIGN GLUED DOWN
PAINTING OVER THE DESIGN

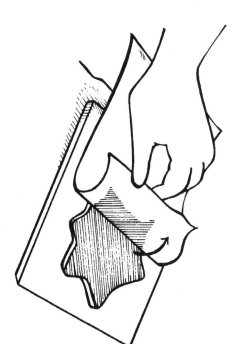

HINT
- Cutting cardboard is very hard for young artists. Offer help as needed.
- Sometimes the paper folds over and sticks to itself when it is peeled from the design. Be sure to use two hands.

PRINTING

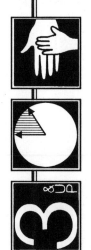

C
L
A
Y

Pressed Play Clay

Materials

play clay (Plasticene) in a variety of colors
2 square sheets of clear plastic Plexiglas 10" x 10"
    (25 cm x 25 cm) or smaller
duct tape for a frame
large paper clip for a hook, optional

Art Process

1. Place one sheet of Plexiglas on the floor.
2. Place little balls and blobs of colored play clay on the sheet of plastic. Place them at random or in a particular design such as flower shapes. Small bits and pinches of clay work best.
3. Take the second sheet of clear plastic and gently place it on top of the clay design.
4. While kneeling over the project, press the sheet of plastic down with both hands on the clay. Watch the colored clay squish, spread, flatten and blend together.
5. Twist, rock, or squish if desired.
6. **Adult** secures the two sheets of plastic together with wide silver duct tape. Tape along all four edges to make a silver frame with the play clay design inside.
7. Unbend a large, heavy paper clip. Insert it through the duct tape to create a hook for hanging the clay picture.

Variation

- Place blobs and drops of paint on a piece of paper. Press a sheet of Plexiglas on the painted paper and watch the design smear, squish, blur, swirl and blend. Peel off the plastic and a pressed paint design will remain on the paper.

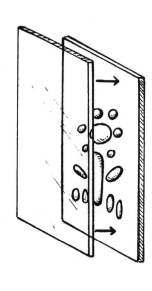

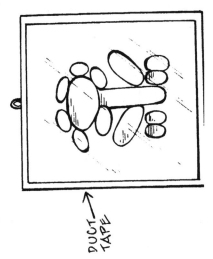

DUCT →
TAPE

HINT
- Be sure the Plexiglas is fairly strong and thick (one-six-teenth to one-eighth inch thick) so it won't snap or break during the pressing stage. Lots of helping hands during the pressing will help prevent the Plexiglas from cracking. Using little balls and piches of clay help, too!

- Instead of saving the pressed clay design, the Plexiglas sheets can be peeled apart and the clay can be scraped off and used again.

Salt Ceramic

Materials

1 cup (200 g) of salt
1/2 cup (100 g) of cornstarch
3/4 cup (180 ml) of water
measuring cups
pan
stove
wooden spoon
piece of aluminum foil

Art Process

1. **Adult** cooks the salt, cornstarch and water over medium heat. Stir constantly with the wooden spoon until the mixture thickens into a big pure white glob. (One batch of this recipe makes a ball the size of a large orange.)
2. **Adult** removes the mixture from the heat.
3. Place the mixture on a piece of foil until cool.
4. Knead thoroughly until soft and pliable.
5. Sculpt any objects or designs. (See suggestions below.)
6. Embed feathers, toothpicks, pebbles or other embellishments while the ceramic is still soft.
7. This material will dry to a rock hardness without baking.

Variations

- For a shiny sculpture, an **adult** can coat finished dry objects with a clear glaze or fingernail polish.
- Some ideas of things to make include: pendants, beads, figures, letters, holiday decorations, items to glue on plaques, play fruit, play vegetables and play cookies.

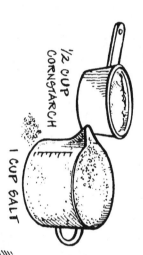

½ CUP CORNSTARCH

1 CUP SALT

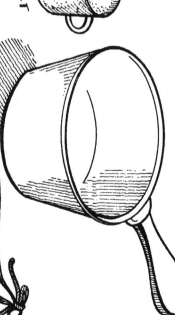

HINT

- Paste food coloring or liquid tempera can be added to the water if colored dough is preferred.
- This recipe keeps in a plastic bag for a few days. Knead the dough before using to restore softness.

caution

4

SCULPTURE

Bottle Bank

Materials

glass bottle or jar (with lid)
small pieces of colored tissue
white glue thinned with water in small dish
paintbrush
table covered with newspaper
block of wood
hammer
screwdriver or chisel

Art Process

1. Remove the lid and stand bottle or jar upside down.
2. Paint a little thinned glue on the jar in one area.
3. Press a piece of tissue into the glue and then paint over the tissue piece with more glue.
4. Continue painting areas with glue and adding more tissue to the glue. Overlap pieces so glass does not show through.
5. Be sure to paint down any edges of tissue with the glue. Bring tissue as close to the opening of the bottle as possible. Do not extend the tissue over the edge or inside the bottle.
6. Dry the project. While drying, an **adult** places the lid on a block of wood, right side up to begin making the slotted lid.
7. Place a screwdriver or a chisel point against the lid and hit the handle with a hammer. This will drive the tool through the lid, making an opening for coins. Hammer several more cuts if necessary to make room for quarters. Sometimes it is necessary to turn the lid over and pound the sharp edges down with the hammer.
8. Screw the lid on the dry bottle and begin saving money.

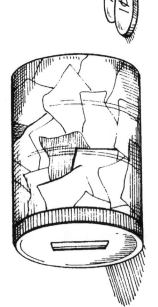

HINT
- Smooth out wrinkles in the tissue with the paintbrush.
- One layer of tissue should be enough. However, young artists like to pile on several layers of tissue paper. If you like, explain that one layer allows more light to shine through the tissue.

caution

CRAFT

Napkin Rings

Materials
cardboard tube (from paper towels or toilet tissue)
knife or scissors
tempera paints
brushes
art tissue paper
liquid starch
clear contact paper
clear gloss enamel, optional

Art Process
1. **Adult** cuts the cardboard tube into sections about two inches (5 cm) in length with a knife or scissors.
2. Paint the sections or rings with a single color of tempera paint to coat. Dry. Apply a second coat.
3. Paint designs on the painted sections or attach pieces of art tissue to the rings with liquid starch.
4. Dry the rings.
5. When dry, an **adult** covers each ring with a strip of clear contact paper to protect napkins from paint or tissue stains.

Variations
• Use felt pens to decorate the rings.
• Cover the rings with papier-mache. Paint the rings when dry.
• Instead of using the contact paper, an **adult** coats the rings with clear gloss enamel for a hard, clear finish.

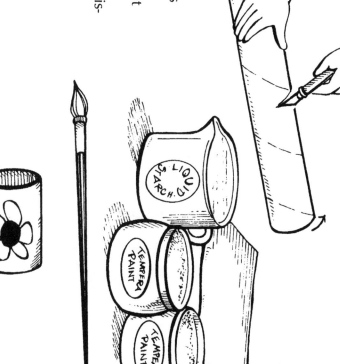

HINT
• Use the napkin rings at meals or snacks.
• Dry rings on a dowel or bottle tops.

C
R
A
F
T

Walking Puppets

Materials
child's drawing
scissors
stiff paper or cardboard
white glue
fingers

Art Process
1. Cut out a drawing and glue it to a piece of stiff paper or cardboard. (Old file folders work well.)
2. With adult help, cut two holes about one quarter inch apart at the base of the drawing. Make each hole large enough to let a finger through.
3. Put two fingers through the holes in the puppet. The fingers become the legs of the puppet.

Variations
• Put one puppet on each hand for a show, story or play.
• Several artists can combine their puppets for a show with several characters.

DRAWING GLUED TO OLD FILE FOLDER

HOLES OUT FOR FINGERS

HINT • Any size or any drawing can be a puppet. It is not necessary for the puppet to be an animal or a person. Even a design can be a puppet.

CRAFT

Metal Cloth Stitchery

Materials

6" x 6" (15 cm x 15 cm) square of metal cloth (sometimes called hardware cloth, available at hardware stores)

yarn, string or embroidery floss

blunt, plastic yarn needle

masking tape

Art Process

1. **Adult** tapes the edges of the hardware cloth with masking tape to prevent hurt fingers.
2. Using a needle strung with yarn, string or floss, push the needle in and out of the holes. Create any patterns or designs.
3. Add other colors.
4. Tie or tape the yarn on the back of the hardware cloth when complete.

Variations

- Other items can be stitched into the design such as old beads, feathers, bits of paper or confetti.
- Pieces of ribbon or lace can be woven through the stitchery if desired.
- A needle is not necessary if the end of the yarn is taped with masking tape to resemble a needle.

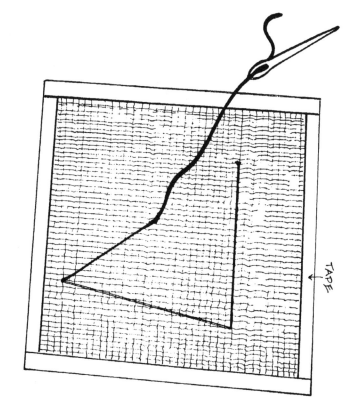

TAPE

HINT

- Metal cloth is a screen with 1/4" holes. It is often used for the tops of hamster cages. An alternative is soffet screen, a more pliable screen on a roll.
- Young artists always have difficulty if the yarn is too long. An arms length of yarn is a good length to use. An adult should be handy to help change yarns or thread needles during the sewing step.

Boiled Paper Treasure Box

caution

Materials
wrapping paper or shelf paper
fabric dye, light color
hot water
pan
stove
cardboard jewelry box
white glue in cup
paintbrush

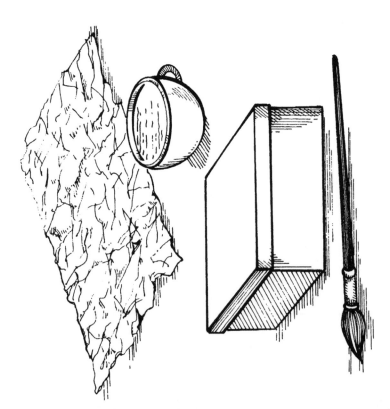

Art Process—Boiled Paper:
1. **Adult** dissolves the dye in hot water in the pan.
2. Crumple up the paper and and add it to the dye. **Adult** boils the die and paper for five minutes.
3. **Adult** rinses the paper in cold water.
4. The artist carefully squeezes out the water from the paper.
5. Spread out the paper to dry on a table or flat surface. The dry paper will look like leather and can be used in any papier-mache project or for the Treasure Box project.

Art Process—Treasure Box:
1. Turn the box and lid upside down.
2. Paint the box with white glue.
3. Cover the box with strips, torn pieces or a large piece of the dry, boiled paper.
4. Place glue on the inside edge of the box.
5. Continue gluing boiled paper over the rim and into the inside of the box. Cover the entire box and lid inside and out. Dry the box.
6. Use this leathery looking box for treasures.

HINT
· The box must be thoroughly dry before placing the lid on top. Sometimes the lid or box edge are so thick that they won't fit back together. Try not to put too much paper on the edge of the box or inside the lid.

C
R
A
F
T

Big Box Sculpture

Materials

cardboard boxes, all shapes and sizes, such as a shoe box,
    milk carton, jewelry box, match box, plastic wrap box,
    paper towel case box, liquor store box or stationery box
cardboard tubes
other paper or cardboard items
white glue
masking tape
scissors
strong yarn
additional collage materials, optional
thick tempera paints with liquid dish soap added
paintbrushes

Art Process

1. Tape boxes and tubes together to make abstract sculptures. Fit
   boxes inside one another; bend boxes to make new shapes; cut
   boxes into new shapes and so on.
2. Use heavy yarn to string boxes together or to hang the sculpture
   from the ceiling.
3. Glue any additional collage materials as desired.
4. Paint the cardboard sculpture. Dry overnight.

Variation

• Instead of an abstract sculpture, make animals or space-age
  cities, cars, rockets, dragons, boats or other inventions or
  machines.

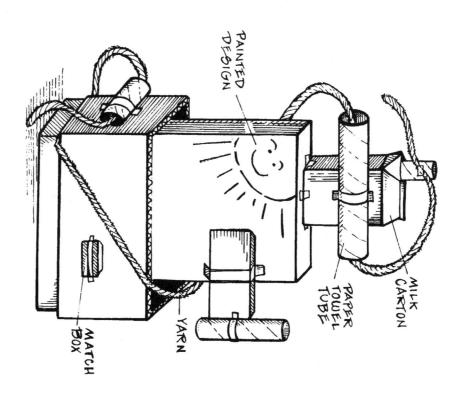

PAINTED DESIGN

MILK CARTON

PAPER TOWEL TUBE

YARN

MATCH BOX

HINT · Adding soap to the paint helps it stick to shiny or slick surfaces and helps paint wash out of clothing and come off hands.

Collection Assemblage

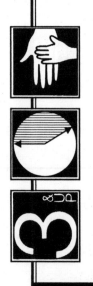

Materials

Collect materials for the assemblage such as colored wire, berry baskets, pizza plates, spools, gift boxes, acorns, pipe cleaners, hole punches, egg cartons, tissue rolls or wrapping paper

white glue
masking tape
cellophane tape
paper clips, paper fasteners
yarn, string
paints and brushes, optional

Art Process

1. Build, assemble, glue and otherwise attach any chosen objects to each other in an assemblage design. An assemblage is like a collage but is more three-dimensional and is made up of a more diverse selection of material.
2. Use tape, glue, paper clips or string to attach materials.
3. Dry the project completely.
4. The artist may decorate or paint the project when complete.

Variations

· Decide on one theme to feature in the assemblage such as Happiness, Spring, Robots, Space or Transportation.
· Use one art medium such as boxes and containers, paper strips, wood scraps or newspaper rolls instead of a large variety of materials.

HINT · A glue gun is a quick-drying alternative to white glue. However, it requires extreme caution and continuous adult supervision at all times. The adult should handle the glue gun with the artist pointing out what needs gluing.

CONSTRUCTION

Foil Treasures

Materials

small three-dimensional items such as golf tees, rubber bands, paper clips, buttons, nuts, bolts, washers, beads or pieces of yarn

old paintbrush

white glue

piece of cardboard

large sheet of heavy duty aluminum foil

tape

Art Process

1. Glue any selection of small objects onto a piece of cardboard.
2. Use an old paintbrush to paint white glue over the entire surface and all of the objects.
3. Carefully place a large sheet of aluminum foil over the raised surface and glued objects.
4. Gently mold and press the foil around the objects to reveal their shapes. Be careful not to tear the foil.
5. Fold excess foil around the back of the cardboard. Tape or glue it in place.

Variation

- For an antique effect, paint the foil with black paint. Before it dries, wipe the paint off, leaving some paint in the creases and wrinkles.

HINT
- Expect the objects to tear through the foil during first attempts with this project. Later attempts will be more controlled.
- Wash the paintbrush thoroughly before the glue dries.

C O N S T R U C T I O N

Coffee Filter Melt

Materials

large coffee filters, opened flat
old crayon stubs without paper, larger crayons
cheese grater
aluminum foil
cookie sheet
oven mitts
wire rack
warm oven, 200 degrees

Art Process

1. Cover the cookie sheet with aluminum foil.
2. Open and press flat two large coffee filters on the cookie sheet.
3. Begin dropping little stubs of old, peeled crayons on the coffee filters.
4. Grate some larger crayons into shavings and drop the shavings on the coffee filters.
5. **Adult** places the cookie sheet in the center of a warm oven.
6. With an adult watching, leave the door of the oven open to watch the crayon begin to melt and soak into the coffee filter. This usually takes only a few minutes. Or close the oven door and turn on the light so the melting can be viewed from the oven window.
7. **Adult** removes the cookie sheet from the oven and places it on a wire rack to cool briefly.
8. Remove the coffee filters and hold up to the light to enjoy the colors.

STEP 4

STEP 3

STEP 2

ALUMINUM FOIL

STEP 1

HINT
· Use an old cheese grater that is no longer needed in the kitchen.
· Save all crayon stubs. Let the artists peel them.

DRAWING

Chalk Flowers

Materials

soft, colored chalk or pastels
colored paper and drawing paper
blossom shapes cut from old file folders
facial tissue
crayons, pencils, felt pens

Art Process

1. Place a blossom shape on the colored paper.
2. Hold the shape with one hand, and with the drawing hand, trace the shape with soft colored chalk.
3. Without letting go of the shape, take a facial tissue and brush the chalk out and away from the shape.
4. When blended and brushed, remove the shape and see the flower left on the paper.
5. Continue moving and tracing with different colors. Tracings can overlap and touch or be spread out on the paper.

Variations

- Simply trace and draw flower shapes instead of brushing them with the tissue.
- Use different shapes of flowers on one design.
- Color or paint the traced shapes. Where shapes overlap, make a new color such as combining red and yellow.
- Use shapes or stencils other than flowers.
- On the same sheet of paper or on a new sheet, trace around the shape with crayon, colored pencil or felt pen.

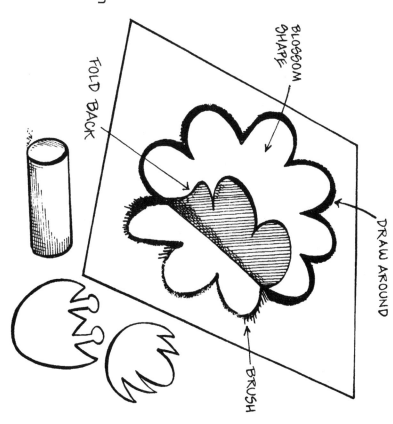

BLOSSOM SHAPE

FOLD BACK

DRAW AROUND

BRUSH

HINT

- Chalk smudges and blurs are typical to this medium. Expect messy hands and elbows.
- One piece of facial tissue should be enough to produce several chalk flowers for each child.
- An **adult** may spray the chalk drawings outside with hair spray or another fixative to reduce smudging.

DRAWING

Encaustic Prints

Materials

objects for printing, such as cookie cutters, plastic toy pieces, rubber stamps, a potato masher, kitchen utensils or cotton swabs

peeled crayons

muffin tin, baking pans

warming tray

assorted paper

Art Process

1. Place one color of peeled crayon in each cup of a muffin tin. Place additional colors in a baking pan, pie pan or other metal pan.

2. Place the muffin tin on a warming tray and melt crayon until it is liquid (usually no more than ten minutes).

3. With **adult** help, dip gadgets, toys or kitchen utensils into the melted crayon. The melted crayon is HOT; supervise this activity closely.

4. Stamp the item quickly on paper before crayon cools and hardens.

5. Dip the item again and continue stamping.

Variation

- Dip an old paintbrush into the melted crayon and paint on paper, rocks or wood.

HINT
- Encaustic is a term which means "painting with melted wax." It resembles the look of oil painting when a brush is used to paint the wax on paper.

- All gadgets, stamps, muffin tins and other printing items will be permanently "crayoned" although they can be washed in hot soapy water with fair results.

- Wear old gloves to protect fingers or use clip-style clothespins to hold gadgets.

D
R
A
W
I
N
G

Salad Spinner

Materials

plastic salad spinner with lid
liquid tempera paints in cups
spoons for each paint color
paper
glitter or confetti, optional

Art Process

1. Cut paper to fit into the bottom of the salad spinner.
2. Place paper in the spinner.
3. Drip paint onto the paper with the spoon. Use more than one color if desired.
4. Snap the lid on the spinner and spin with the handle.
5. Open and add glitter or confetti as desired.

Variation

• Think of other spinning ideas, such as an old record player or a lazy susan. Experiment with paint, felt pens and crayons.

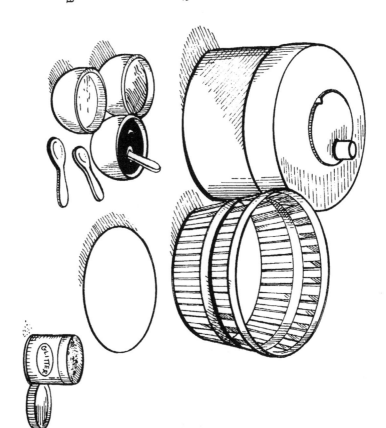

HINT
• Younger children may need help spinning.
• Prepare a drying area such as newspaper on the floor near the project.
• This project is very messy to carry so have soapy water in a bucket ready for hand washing.

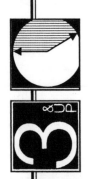

Paint Crayons

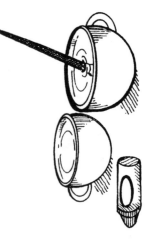

Materials
paint crayons
water in cups
paper
paintbrushes, optional

Art Process
1. Paint crayons can be found at school supply, art or hobby stores. They are a watercolor base paint in crayon shape.
2. Dip the paint crayon into a small dish of water.
3. Draw with the moistened paint crayon on the paper.
4. Or use a wet paintbrush to paint on the paint crayon marks, creating additional designs.
5. Dry the painting.

Variations
- Experiment with different textures and colors of papers.
- Make paint crayons by making a thick mixture of dry tempera paint and water, pour into a muffin tin and dry. Draw with the dry paint like a crayon or dip the dried muffin of paint into a cup of water as described above.

HINT
- Be sure to keep water dishes refilled with clean water for the brightest designs. Artists should be encouraged to change their own water.
- Do not leave the paint crayons soaking in the dish of water or they will dissolve and disintegrate.

P A I N T I N G

Roller Fence Painting

Materials

outdoor fence
large trays
different types of paint rollers
tempera paint
large sheets of butcher paper
masking tape
clean-up materials (bucket, water and rags)

Art Process

1. With masking tape, secure a large sheet of butcher paper to an outdoor fence.
2. Fill trays with different colors of tempera paint.
3. Roll paint rollers in trays of paint.
4. Roll paint on the butcher paper.

Variations

- Use a wall or door if a fence is not available. (Cover floor with newspapers.)
- Put textured surfaces under the paper before rolling paint over the paper.
- Do this project on a paint easel instead of a fence.

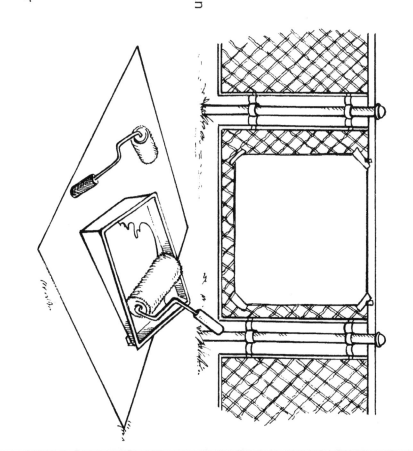

HINT
- Do not do this project on the floor or artists will end up crawling through paint.
- The fence materials will show through the painting, picking up the textures of wire or wood.
- Have clean up-materials handy.

P A I N T I N G

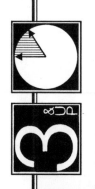

Glitter Paint Shake

Materials

matte board or cardboard
white glue, thinned with water in a cup
paintbrushes
salt or cheese shakers with large holes
powdered tempera paint
glitter

Art Process

1. Paint the entire surface of the matte board or cardboard with thinned white glue.
2. Fill shakers with powdered tempera and glitter.
3. Shake the paint glitter mixture onto the glue.
4. Dry the project for a long time.

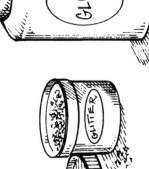

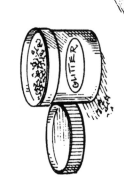

HINT
· Powdered tempera can be inhaled. It is a good idea to wear paint filter masks or doctor's masks while shaking the powdered paint. Artists enjoy this.

· This project takes a long time to dry, so have a shelf or drying area where it can remain undisturbed for several days.

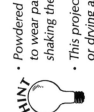

PAINTING

Salty Paint Shake

Materials
bag of table salt
powdered tempera paints
containers (margarine or yogurt)
white glue in small jars
paintbrushes
trays
salt shakers
paper

Art Process
1. With adult help, mix salt with powdered tempera paint in a container.
2. Put the colored salt into a salt shaker.
3. Make additional colors for other salt shakers.
4. Paint a design on the paper with a paintbrush dipped in white glue.
5. Shake the colored salt from the shaker on the glue design.
6. Shake excess salt onto the tray to be used again.

Variation
- Use white beach sand instead of salt. Sand can be purchased in bags at a hardware store or brought home from the seashore or river.

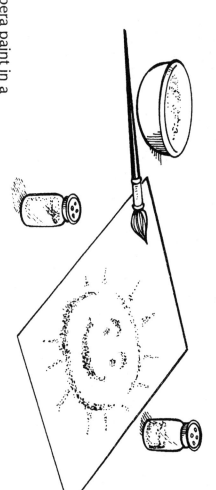

HINT
- Some children do better squeezing the white glue out of a glue bottle instead of painting it on the paper.
- Instead of shakers, younger children may control the colored salt better when a plastic tub is filled with about one inch of colored sand. The artist can use hands to pour sand on the glue design. Pour extra sand back into the tub. This gives a thicker coloration and design.

PAINTING

Bubble Prints

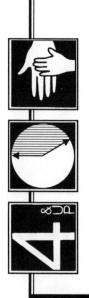

Materials

paper
tempera paint
liquid detergent
water

quart container
stirring stick or spoon
shallow aluminum cake pan
straight straws (not flexible)

Art Process

1. The night before the activity, mix one-third cup tempera paint with one-third cup liquid detergent in a quart container.
2. Add water to fill the container and stir.
3. If several colors are desired, make a separate quart solution for each one.
4. Leave the contents sitting overnight.
5. The next day, pour the paint mixture into a shallow cake pan.
6. **Adult** demonstrates how to safely blow through a straw without sucking in. Let the artist press a piece of paper gently onto the bubbles. The bubbles will pop and leave an imprint on the paper.
7. Next, the artists can experiment with bubble blowing and pressing the paper into the bubbles to achieve a bubble print or design.

Variations

- Use various papers for different printing results.
- Instead of paint, blow bubbles in a pan of detergent and water only. When the bubbles are thick and high, add some drops of food coloring on the bubbles. Slowly lower a paper plate or piece of paper onto the bubbles and a print of the bubbles will be left on the paper.

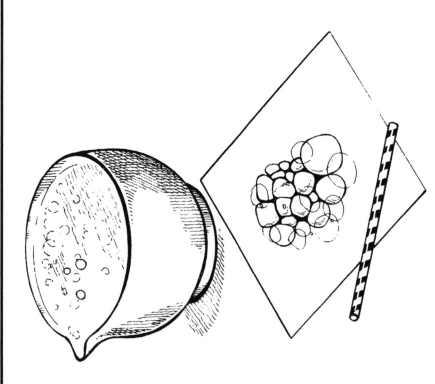

HINT
- *Cut a little nick or hole near the blowing end of the straw to help prevent artists from sucking up soapy solution into the mouth.*
- *For lasting, strong bubbles, add a few tablespoons of sugar to the quart solution.*

PAINTING

Claydoh Beads

Materials

3/4 cup (150 g) flour
1/2 cup (100 g) cornstarch
1/2 cup (100 g) salt
powdered tempera or powdered vegetable dye (p. 27) for color
3/8 cup (90 ml) warm water
bowl
toothpicks
string, yarn or leather strings
clear gloss enamel, optional

Art Process

1. Mix flour, cornstarch and salt in a bowl. (Add powdered tempera or powdered vegetable dye for colored dough.)
2. Add warm water slowly until mixture can be kneaded into a stiff dough.
3. Add flour to reduce stickiness if necessary.
4. Roll dough into balls for beads.
5. Poke a hole in each ball with a toothpick and dry for a few days. (Large beads take longer to dry.)
6. Paint if desired.
7. **Adult** coats the beads with a clear gloss enamel if desired.
8. When the beads are dry, string them on yarn, string or leather strips. You may tie knots in between each bead.

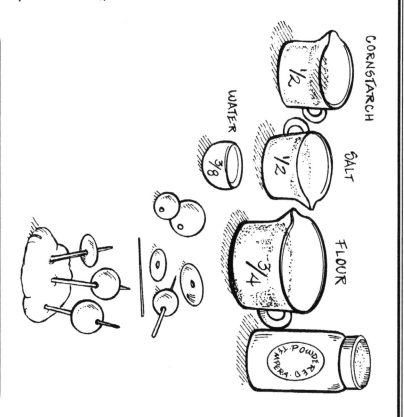

CORNSTARCH · SALT · FLOUR
1/2 · 1/2 · 3/4
WATER 3/8
POWDERED TEMPERA

HINT

- To dry beads, stick toothpicks into a ball of play-dough. Place one bead on each toothpick. Twist beads on toothpicks during the drying time to be sure they don't stick to the toothpicks.
- This recipe makes a fairly smooth dough that keeps its color when dry.
- A bit of salt residue shows in the beads, especially in darker colored doughs.

Edible Sculpting Dough

Materials

bowl and spoon
measuring cups and spoons
1 package dry yeast
1-1/2 cups (345 ml) very warm water
1 egg
1/4 cup (60 ml) honey
1/4 cup (50 g) shortening
5 cups (1000 g) flour
baking sheet
towel
1 teaspoon salt
350 degree oven
oven mitts

Art Process

1. Mix the yeast and very warm water in a bowl.
2. Add the egg, honey, shortening and salt.
3. Slowly add the flour until a ball of dough forms. Add a little more flour if the dough is too sticky.
4. Knead the dough by hand on a floured board.
5. Begin sculpting making only flat figures since the dough will rise.
6. Cover the sculptures with a towel and place in a warm place for about one-half hour to rise. For very puffy sculptures, let the dough rise longer.
7. Bake at 350 degrees for twenty minutes or until golden brown.
8. Eat sculptures or save as is.

Variation

- Insert a paper clip into the dough before baking and the sculpture will have a hook for displaying the sculpture. Loop some yarn, ribbon or colorful embroidery floss through the paper clip to hang the sculpture from a tree, nail or doorknob.

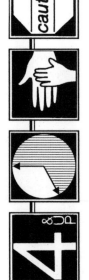

HINT
· If sculptures sound hollow when tapped with the handle of a table knife, this is a good indication that they are baked and ready to remove from the oven.

· Experiment with a garlic press and other tools to make decorations for the sculpture.

D O U G H

Tissue Mobile

Materials

yarn, 1 yard (1 m) long
art tissue or white tissue
glue mixture in cup—two parts white glue to one part liquid starch
needle and thread
coat hanger
watercolor paints, optional

Art Process

1. Tie the ends of the string of yarn together.
2. Dip the yarn in the cup of glue mixture. Run fingers down the yarn to squeeze out the excess mixture.
3. Place the sticky yarn on a piece of art tissue or white tissue in any shape.
4. Place a second piece of tissue on top of the yarn and gently press where the yarn touches tissue.
5. Dry the project overnight.
6. The following day, cut around the outside of the yarn shape.
7. Paint on the white tissue with watercolors if desired.
8. Poke a needle and thread through the edge of the tissue next to the inside of the yarn.
9. Hang one or many of these shapes from a coat hanger. If the shape was painted, it can dry while hanging.

Variations

• This project makes nice holiday ornaments.
• The mobile looks pretty hanging in windows where light can shine through it.

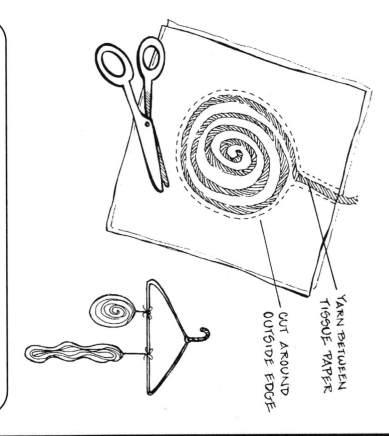

YARN BETWEEN TISSUE PAPER

CUT AROUND OUTSIDE EDGE

HINT

• When squeezing the excess glue from the yarn, pull gently. If pulled too hard, the yarn will stretch, spring out of control and flip glue everywhere.
• An adult may have to help with placing the second sheet of tissue on the yarn and possibly with the cutting step.
• An adult should have the needle and thread ready to go and may need to help with this step.

S
C
U
L
P
T
U
R
E

4
PC&8

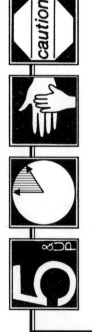

Soap Sculpture

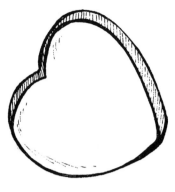

Materials
bar of soap
small, fairly sharp knife
other sculpting tools such as a screw driver, spoon,
    toothpick or clay tools
newspaper

Art Process
1. Artists who know how to use a knife safely can do this activity with close adult supervision.
2. Draw the outline of an object on the bar of soap. Select a fairly simple shape without details or intricacies.
3. Use a knife or other tools to sculpt and cut away the soap.
4. To smooth edges or cut sides, rub a wet finger over the spot.
5. Enjoy as a sculpture, or use as a fancy guest soap.

Variation
- See p. 47 for the directions of how to make Soap Clay which can also be molded or carved.

HINT · Observe caution and supervision with carving. It's a good idea to have a way to brace the sculpture while carving it. For instance, place the soap up against a block of wood which is nailed into another board.

S
C
U
L
P
T
U
R
E

Sprinkle Collage

Materials

white glue in squeeze bottle
paper
sprinkles such as glitter, confetti, seeds or pine needles
tray or container for excess sprinkles

Art Process

1. Squeeze a small bottle of white glue over a piece of paper to
   make a glue design.
2. Sprinkle the wet glue design with any or all of the sprinkles.
3. Curve the paper and dump excess sprinkles into a container to
   use for another sprinkle design.
4. Dry the project completely.

Variation

· Other materials for sprinkling include wood shavings, sawdust,
  salt, powdered tempera, sand, or bits of yarn.

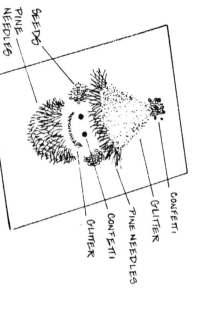

SEEDS
PINE
NEEDLES
CONFETTI
GLITTER
PINE NEEDLES
CONFETTI
GLITTER

GLITTER

GLUE

HINT
· Some children can dribble glue from a stick or straw
  onto the paper better than controlling a squeeze
  bottle.
· Pouring or dumping the excess sprinkles can be
  tricky, but let the artist try before an adult takes over
  the job.

Confetti Explosion

Materials

confetti, paper or metallic
holes from paper punch
white glue in bottle
black paper

Art Process

1. Draw a design with glue on the black paper.
2. Sprinkle confetti into the glue design. Place confetti and dots one at a time in glue, or sprinkle confetti and dots all over the glue all at once.
3. Dry the project completely.

Variations

- Use bits of tissue, cotton balls, beads or other collage items instead of confetti.
- Fill a cookie pan about one-quarter inch deep with confetti. Make a glue design on paper, turn the paper over and press the paper into the confetti. Turn right side up and dry.
- Place a glue design in the bottom of a tub of confetti. Scoop confetti over the glue design. Shake off the excess confetti. Dry the project completely.

HINT
- Use a damp cotton swab to lift a piece of confetti and place it on the glue design. This makes placing individual pieces of confetti easier than trying to pick them up by hand.
- If creating a larger design, work on small parts one at a time, so glue doesn't dry out

COLLAGE

Feeling Tree

Materials

finger paintings in brown, green or any colors
cupcake liners
colored scraps of paper and tissue
collage items for a nest such as straw or grass, rolls of newspaper, yarn or Easter grass
scissors
tape
glue
wall or large piece of paper taped to the wall

Art Process

1. Cut brown finger paintings into sections of a tree trunk and tree branches. Tape them to the wall forming a large tree.
2. Cut green finger paintings into leaves and tape them to the brown tree.
3. Add cupcake liners and other scraps of paper for blossom and tape them to the tree.
4. Use collage items to make a nest. For example, little rolls of newspaper resemble sticks. Tape or glue it next to the tree.
5. From scraps of paper, cut out birds, eggs or baby birds and tape in the nest.
6. Add other things to the tree such as caterpillars, butterflies, realistic or imaginary bugs...even a kite!

Variation

· Build a big house and yard with lots of things in the windows or a river filled with fish and boats or under the sea with amazing creatures, plants and fish.

HINT · Collage is an exciting technique for building and creating a picture that can both be seen and felt–a "feeling picture."

· Be prepared to see quite unusual things in the tree as young artists have a their own perception of trees and nature.

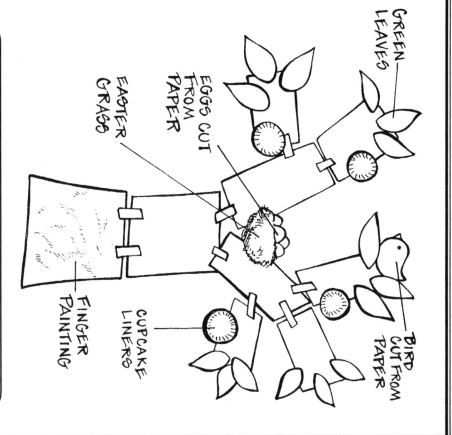

GREEN LEAVES

EGGS CUT FROM PAPER

EASTER GRASS

FINGER PAINTING

CUPCAKE LINERS

BIRD CUT FROM PAPER

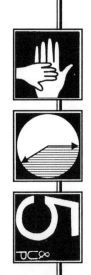

C
O
L
L
A
G
E

Treasure Strings

Materials
heavy yarn
plastic needle
items for stringing such as sections of tissue rolls, styrofoam pieces, hole-punched paper scraps, foil, egg carton cups, sections of straws, pieces of colored paper, spools or buttons

Art Process
1. Knot the far end of the yarn to keep the objects from sliding off. Sometimes it helps to knot one item into the knot to form a barrier to help begin stringing.
2. String any objects onto the yarn in a random or a planned pattern.
3. Add more yarn if desired to make a very long necklace or a garland to decorate the windows, walls or doorways.
4. Make a necklace, bracelet, belt or hanging.

Variation
· Plan a theme or specific types of items for the project such as: beads from old jewelry and foil scraps; paper circles and straw pieces; flower shapes and tissue sections or toys and puzzle pieces.

HINT · Young artists usually need help with threading yarn in the plastic needle and with knotting the end of the yarn.
· If the plastic needle won't go through some papers or items, an adult can make holes with a hole punch, a sharp pencil or scissor point.

Fabric Note Pad

Materials

inexpensive, small note pad

rectangular piece of heavy cardboard or thin wood measuring twice as large or more as the note pad

fabric scraps cut in small squares and other shapes

scraps of rickrack, lace, ribbon and other notions

wall hanging hooks

white glue in dish, slightly thinned with water

white glue in bottle

paintbrush

small dried flowers, optional

paper fastener

    piece of string

    pencil

    knife

Art Process

1. Glue scraps of fabric all over the piece of cardboard or wood using a brush and the thinned glue. Use plenty of glue. The fabric can be soaked through and will dry nicely later.

2. Glue rickrack, lace or other notions around the border. Dry the project overnight.

3. When dry, glue the note pad to the center of the decorated cardboard or wood.

4. Glue a bit of dried flowers to the note pad board, if desired.

5. **Adult** pokes a hole with a pencil or the point of a knife in the cardboard. Stick a paper fastener through the hole. Wrap one end of string around the paper fastener.

6. **Adult** cuts a groove with a knife into the top end of a pencil and tie the other end of the string around the pencil groove. The pencil will hang on a string next to the note pad, ready to go to work.

caution

5 C&8

STEP 1

FRONT   BACK

STEP 2

SEQUINS   TRIM

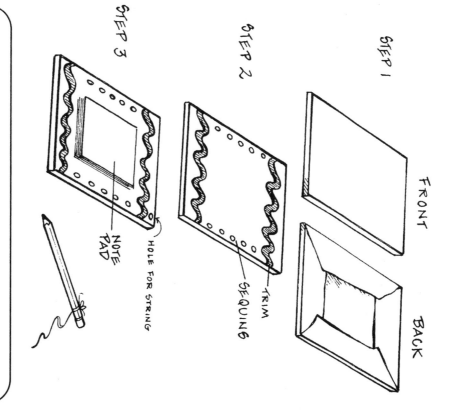

STEP 3

NOTE PAD

HOLE FOR STRING

HINT
- Glue will hold best if allowed to dry completely.
- With one-on-one adult supervision, a glue gun can be used by the adult to glue the artist's work or ideas.

Sea Scene

Materials

two paper plates per artist

felt pens and crayons

colored cellophane or art tissue

scissors

white glue

yarn

stapler

plastic wrap

sand

Art Process

1. With adult help, cut away the center of one paper plate, leaving the rim.

2. Turn the rim right side up and put glue along the inside edge.

3. Stretch a piece of clear plastic over the opening and glue it down, creating a window effect. Cut away excess plastic when dry.

4. Color and cut out little fish, shells and other sea creatures from the center piece of the plate.

5. Glue fish, yarn, sand, cellophane or tissue onto the second plate.

6. Place the plate rim upside down on the full plate and staple around the outside.

7. Decorate the rim further if desired.

Variation

- Make other scenes on paper plates such as any interesting collage, family portraits, treasure displays or pressed and dried flowers.

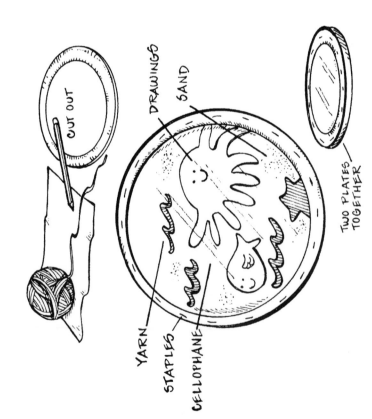

CUT OUT

DRAWINGS

SAND

YARN

STAPLES

CELLOPHANE

TWO PLATES TOGETHER

HINT
- The plastic covered rim looks like a window peering into a fish bowl or aquarium.
- Artists usually need help controlling the plastic wrap and the stapler.
- An adult can use a glue gun for one-on-one gluing of the rim to the second plate. As always, observe caution around a glue gun.

CONSTRUCTION

Summer

Sand Drawing

Materials

trip to seashore, river or large sandy area (a dusty-dirt playground also works)
bare feet, fingers
long stick, other drawing tools
water in bucket or from hose, optional

Art Process

1. Go to a large, open sandy beach or dusty-dirt play area.
2. Remove shoes and socks.
3. Begin making marks in the sand or dirt by scooting and shuffling bare feet through the sand or dirt. Use fingers, hands, shells, a long stick or other tools to draw in the sand or dirt.
4. If the sand or dirt is too dry for a clear impression, add water and moisten the drawing area. Then begin to draw in the moistened sand or dirt.
5. Leave the drawing when complete or smooth the dirt or sand with a leafy branch, hands or even a broom.

Variations

• Make a footprint trail for others to follow.
• Write names or messages in the sand or dirt.
• Add sculpture items such as rocks or leaves collected from the surrounding area to enhance the drawing.

HINT • Have towels on hand to clean sandy toes before putting shoes back on.
• Be prepared for sandy hands and artists who want to wade in the water.

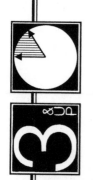

D
R
A
W
I
N
G

Shadow Drawing

Materials
large sheet of butcher paper
felt pens, paints and brushes, crayon or chalk
sunny day outside
4 rocks, optional

Art Process
1. Go for a walk looking for shadows on the ground.
2. Find a shadow that is appealing in design.
3. Place the large sheet of butcher paper on the shadow. Adjust the paper so that the shadow is captured on the paper.
4. If the day is windy, place a rock on each corner of the paper to keep it from blowing away.
5. Using any choice of drawing or painting tools, trace, outline, color in or decorate the paper using the shadow as the design.
6. When complete, remove the paper and observe the shadow drawing.

Variations
- Cut the design out and glue it on another sheet of paper contrasting in color. Black is often an effective choice for a background.
- When using crayon, place textured surfaces behind the paper to add design to the shadow drawing. A wire mesh screen, sheet of plywood, bumpy scrap of vinyl flooring or scrap of formica make interesting textures.
- Make a shadow drawing of a friend's shadow.

HINT
- Crayons take a long time on this design activity, but some children enjoy this. Crayons also tend to poke holes in the paper so it helps to have cardboard or a sheet of plywood under the paper as a hard surface.
- Paint covers fastest. Carry cups of paints and paint-brushes in a flat cardboard box to prevent spilling.

D R A W I N G

Big Blot

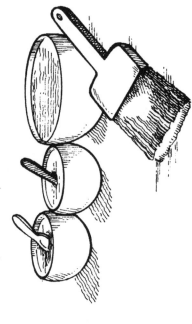

Materials

big sheet of butcher paper
spoon or large paintbrush
liquid tempera paints in containers
newspaper

Art Process

1. Fold paper in half. Open it.
2. Spoon or brush paints mainly on the fold line.
3. Refold and press the paper out from the fold to the edge to move and mix the paints.
4. Open the painting.
5. Carry the Big Blot to a drying area where the painting can dry flat on newspapers. Dry it completely.

Variation

- When the Big Blot is dry, some children enjoy cutting out the Big Blot shape. This can be displayed as is or glued to another backing in a complementary color.

FOLD

HINT

- *Younger children will need the paper pre-folded and may need assistance with unfolding the large paper.*

- *The main appeal of this art experience is the size of the blot. It might help children if they make the traditional small blot on smaller folded paper first so they understand the concept of what they are making.*

PAINTING

Fence Mural

Materials

long fence
roll of wide, heavy paper
tape
stapler
paint mixed in cans or wide bowls
paintbrushes
small tables, chairs or boxes, optional
bucket of soapy water and rags for clean up

Art Process

1. Tape or staple a long, wide, heavy roll of paper to a fence. Use lots of tape or staples so the paper will not tear and fall down.
2. Place containers of paints and brushes at intervals along the fence. Small tables, flat chairs or strong cardboard boxes work well as paint stands.
3. Several artists can paint at the same time on the same long piece of paper.

Variations

- Make up a play and use the mural for a backdrop or scenery. Layer several murals which can be changed for different scenes.
- A group of artists could agree on a theme and paint a scene together. Some suggestions are Houses in Our Neighborhood, Dinosaur World, Wild and Bright Colors, Around the World, Summer Fun or The World's Biggest Painting.

HINT

- Free roll-ends of heavy paper are often available from newspaper printers.
- Fence murals make great group or party activities.
- Paint will drip down the paper using this method which can be improved by mixing paints fairly thick and adding liquid starch for smoothness.

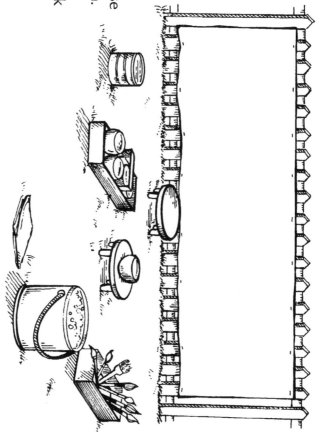

Flicker Paint

Materials
white drawing paper
water
sponge
watercolor paints
paintbrush

Art Process
1. Cover both sides of white drawing paper with a water filled sponge.
2. Fill paintbrush with watercolor paint and drip drops of paint on the paper.
3. Flick or shake the paint on the paper too.
4. Continue painting this way with other colors.
5. Colors will blend and mix on the wet paper.
6. Let paintings dry in place rather than moving them inside.

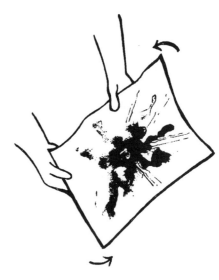

COVER BOTH SIDES

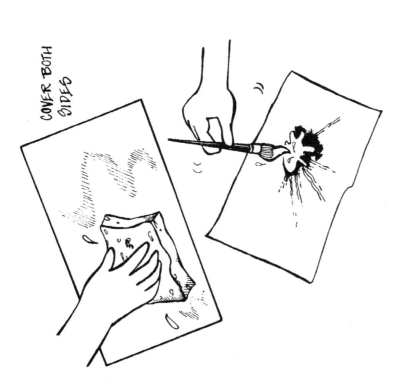

HINT
- Do this project outside on the grass so flicking the paint will not spot walls. Set rocks on corners of paper so it won't blow away.
- Wear old clothes or cover clothing with a BIG shirt with sleeves cut off to elbow length.
- Have a soapy bucket of water handy for cleaning up faces and hands.

P A I N T I N G

Spray Painting

Materials
heavy white paper
tempera paints mixed to a medium consistency
paintbrushes
spray bottle filled with water (set on spray, not stream)

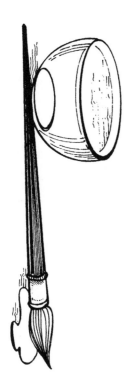

Art Process
1. Place the heavy white paper outdoors on a flat surface such as the grass or inside on a covered floor.
2. Drip paint from brushes onto the paper.
3. Spray clear water from the spray bottle on the drops of paint.
4. Paint drops will thin, spread and mix.

Variation
- Sprinkle dry tempera paint on heavy butcher paper and spray with water. Do this project on a rainy day and carry outside into the rain to moisten.

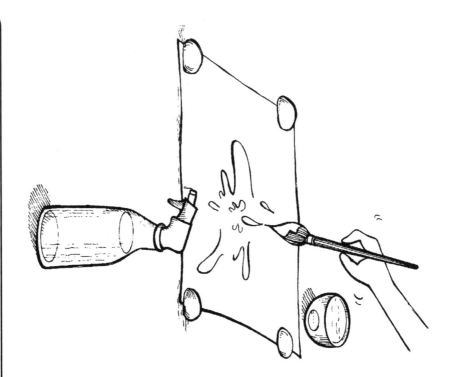

HINT
- This is a good outdoor project which leaves plenty of room to "spray."
- Try hanging the paper on a fence so that all the paint runs down. Dry the project on the fence before removing.

PAINTING

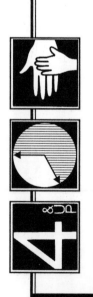

Earth Clay Explore

Materials

earth clay, sometimes called moist clay (available at craft shops, art supply stores and school supply stores)

tools such as cookie cutters, garlic press, knives, nails, toy pieces, a spatula, rolling pin, blocks or toothpicks

table covered with a heavy garbage bag

tape

covered artist

Art Process

1.. Protect the work area with a heavy garbage bag taped down to the table.
2. Roll, squeeze, pound, press and form earth clay in any manner desired.
3. Dry the clay objects if the artist wishes to save the work. If not, return the clay to the airtight container to use again later.

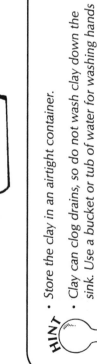

HINT · Store the clay in an airtight container.

· Clay can clog drains, so do not wash clay down the sink. Use a bucket or tub of water for washing hands and utensils. Discard the water outside.

· This is a messy activity, but a very rewarding and artistically satisfying project

C
L
A
Y

Earth Clay Sculpture

Materials

earth clay, sometimes called moist clay (available at craft shops,
   art supply stores and school supply stores)
rolling pin or cylinder block
other tools including a spatula, nails, cookie cutters, garlic press or
   knives
tempera paints
paintbrushes
clear gloss enamel or lacquer, optional

Art Process

1. Roll out a small portion of earth clay about one-half inch thick.
2. Cut out any shape such as a fish, a circle, a square, a heart or a
   leaf.
3. Decorate the shape with designs pressed or cut into the clay.
4. Dry the clay.
5. Paint designs onto the clay shape.
6. When dry, an adult can paint the clay shape with clear gloss
   enamel or lacquer.

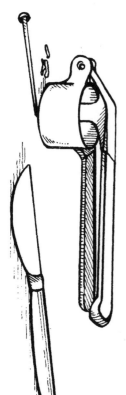

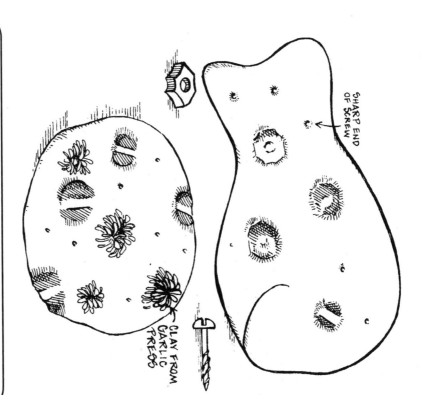

SHARP END OF SCREW

CLAY FROM GARLIC PRESS

HINT

- Protect the work area with a heavy garbage bag taped down to the table.
- Store clay in an airtight container.
- Clay can clog drains, so do not wash clay down the sink. Use a bucket or tub of water for washing hands and utensils. Discard the water outside.

C
L
A
Y

Bowling

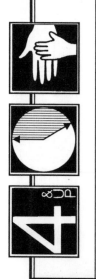

Materials

plastic juice bottles
double sheet of newspaper for each bottle
sand or rice
funnel
newspaper torn in strips
wallpaper paste
yarn

paint
paintbrushes
white glue
collage materials
clear gloss enamel or polymer

Art Process

1. Crumple a double sheet of newspaper into a round shape to make a head on a bottle. Pull out a section for the neck to stick into the bottle.

2. Fill each plastic bottle about one-third full with sand or rice using the funnel. (This will keep bottles from tipping over too easily.)

3. Paste newspaper strips all over the head and down onto the neck of the bottle and all over the entire bottle if desired. Dry the project several days.

4. Paint decorations on the bottles such as eyes, a nose and a mouth. Add yarn for hair. The artist may also choose to paint the bottle using bright colors, shapes and designs. Decorate with collage materials if desired. Dry the project completely.

5. **Adult** paints the bowling bottle with clear gloss enamel or polymer. Dry again.

6. To bowl, set up the bottles at the end of a room. Mark off the floor with masking tape for an alley. Roll soft balls or any other balls down the alley and see how many bottles can be knocked down.

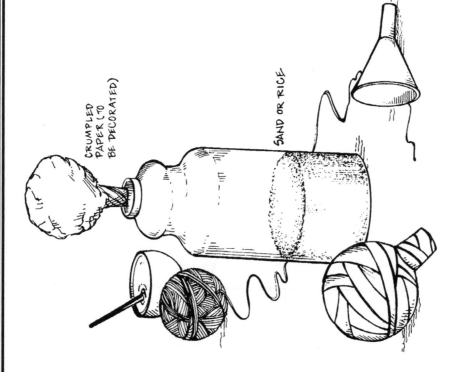

CRUMPLED PAPER (TO BE DECORATED)

SAND OR RICE

HINT · Keep in mind that the bottles can lose their "heads", the paint may chip off or other disasters if the children throw too hard or the alley is too long. Start small for the bowling and realize that most children will naturally overdo the throwing.

S
C
U
L
P
T
U
R
E

Fence Weaving

Materials

fence (chain link fences work well)

items for weaving such as crepe paper, strips of fabric, rope, ribbon, lace, strips of newsprint, other paper or yarn

Art Process

1. Find a fence that is comfortable to reach and easy to stand beside.
2. Weave and wrap materials through the fence.
3. Continue adding decorations and weaving until the fence is woven and decorated as desired.
4. Remove the weaving before it rains, but enjoy it as long as possible.

Variations

· Make a swing-set or playground equipment weaving.
· Plan the fence weaving as part of a party, play or special event.

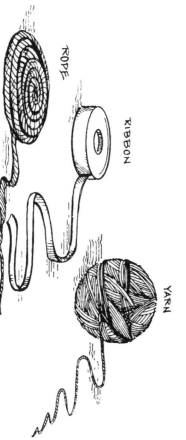

ROPE

RIBBON

YARN

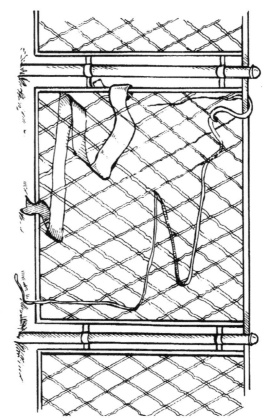

HINT · One trick to making weaving easier for young artists is to keep the strips fairly short (not more than two to three feet in length).

· Another more challenging weaving approach is to roll the strips in a ball and place them in a container with a hole at the top. The artist feeds the strips through the fence wire, unrolling it from the container.

S C U L P T U R E

Brick Making

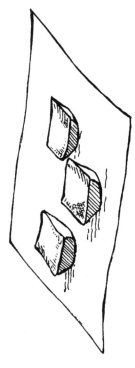

Materials

dirt
water
plastic bucket
muffin tins or ice cube trays

Art Process

1. Put dirt in a plastic bucket and mix in just enough water to form a mud ball.
2. Press the mud into muffin tin cups or ice cube tray sections.
3. Place the tins or trays in a warm place for about ten days, or bake at 250 degrees for fifteen minutes.
4. When cool, drop the "bricks" on newsprint on the floor and see which ones break and which ones hold together. Use the solid bricks for building.
5. Make as many bricks as possible for the most fun in building.

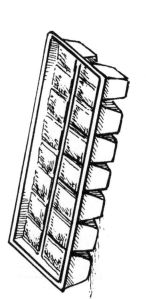

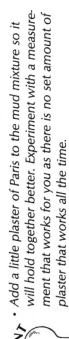

HINT
- Add a little plaster of Paris to the mud mixture so it will hold together better. Experiment with a measurement that works for you as there is no set amount of plaster that works all the time.
- Follow the building suggestions for Brick Building (page 245).

caution

Brick Building

Materials

homemade dirt bricks (see Brick Making, page 244)
rocks, stones or gravel
sticks and weeds
plaster of Paris or mud

Art Process

1. Attach bricks and other items together in a free-form building using plaster of Paris mixed to a runny consistency for the "cement." Mud also works to stick the items together.
2. Dip, paint or spoon plaster over the items and add them to the building.
3. Dry the project overnight or longer.

Variations

- Build with wood scraps and glue.
- Build with sugar cubes and Royal Icing Art (page 127).

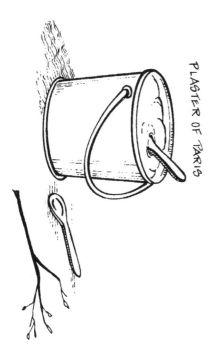

PLASTER OF PARIS

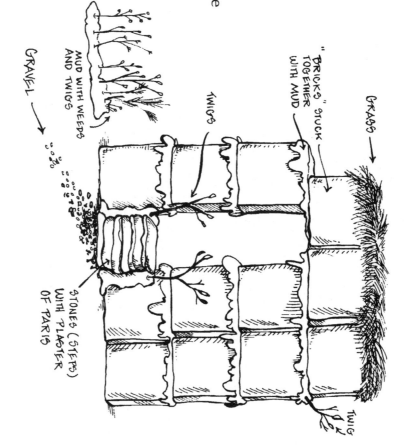

GRASS →

"BRICKS" STUCK TOGETHER WITH MUD

TWIGS

MUD WITH WEEDS AND TWIGS

GRAVEL →

STONES (STEPS) WITH PLASTER OF PARIS

TWIG

HINT
- Keep a soapy bucket and towels nearby for clean up.
- Some children really do not like to get their hands dirty; sometimes this is merely a stage. Be understanding. This project is not for everyone.

Basket Stitching

Materials

loosely woven small cane basket
yarns in many colors
plastic darning needles
scissors

Art Process

1. Thread a darning needle with a fairly long piece of yarn. Use double yarn tied at one end for younger children.
2. Begin stitching the yarn through the holes in the basket in any random or planned design. Be very cautious of space between artists so no one gets poked with a needle.
3. Change colors as desired.

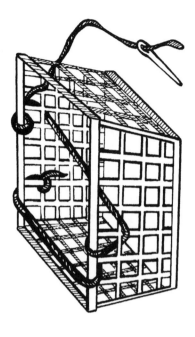

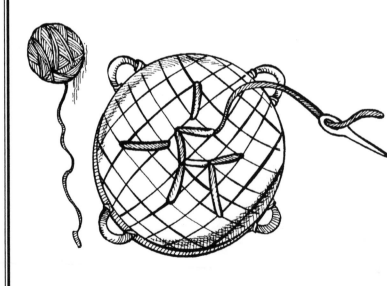

HINT
- The firmness of the basket makes it easy for young children to hold and push the needle through the basket.
- The inexpensive baskets that hold paper plates work well.
- Children always seem to need help with threading, tying and sometimes starting or ending the stitching.

Pressed Flower Frames

Materials

fresh flowers
newspapers
heavy books
glue in squeeze bottle
scissors
pen

wooden curtain rings
heavy paper
scrap paper
white glue in a dish
toothpicks to dip in glue

Art Process

Drying

Place fresh flowers on the newspaper. Flowers should not be touching each other. Put several layers of newspaper on top of the flowers. Lay heavy books on top of the newspaper and flowers. Bricks or other heavy objects also work well. Leave the flowers undisturbed for about four weeks to dry completely. (Thick flowers will take longer.)

Framing

1. Place a curtain ring on a piece of paper and draw around the outside of the ring. Cut the circle a little smaller than the drawn circle.
2. Choose a pressed flower and turn it upside down on the circle of paper. Dip the end of the toothpick into the glue and dot it lightly to the back of the flower. Carefully lift the flower and place it glue side down on the paper circle. Repeat until the desired flower design is complete.
3. Apply glue to the back of the curtain ring from a squeeze bottle. Lift the ring and stick it to the paper circle containing the flowers. Keep the screw eye of the ring at the top. Dry the project completely.
4. The ring becomes a frame for the flower arrangement, and the screw eye can be used as a wall hook.

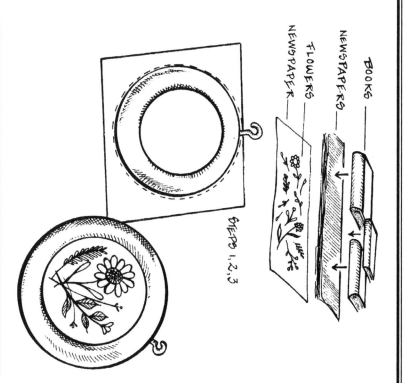

BOOKS
NEWSPAPERS
FLOWERS
NEWSPAPER

STEPS 1, 2, 3

HINT
- Pressed and dried flowers are delicate and need to be handled with care.
- Press flowers a month ahead of time so they are ready for this project.
- Young artists can do this project on their own, but assistance will likely be necessary with the gluing of the ring to the paper. Even if this project doesn't turn out "adult-like," allow creativity to move at the child's pace.

C
R
A
F
T

Parade

Materials

tricycles, bikes, big wheels, scooters or wagons

decorating materials including crepe paper, balloons, tin cans, aluminum pie plates, flags, streamers, yarn and string

masking tape

Art Process

1. Decorate tricycles or other riding or pulling toys for a parade.
2. Some decorating ideas are:
   - weave crepe paper through bicycle spokes
   - tie balloons or streamers to handle bars
   - make a float in a wagon
   - hang noisy cans or pie plates from bikes
3. Start a parade around the playground, park or down the neighborhood sidewalks.
4. Add marching people (decorate them too!), rhythm instruments or noise makers to the parade.

Variations

- Parades can have a holiday or celebration theme.
- Invite pets to join the parade.
- March to music from a tape recorder.

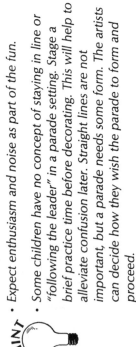

BALLOONS

STREAMERS

ALUMINUM
PIE PLATE ON A DOWEL

YARN

CREPE PAPER
TAPED DOWN

HINT
- Expect enthusiasm and noise as part of the fun.
- Some children have no concept of staying in line or "following the leader" in a parade setting. Stage a brief practice time before decorating. This will help to alleviate confusion later. Straight lines are not important, but a parade needs some form. The artists can decide how they wish the parade to form and proceed.

CONSTRUCTION

Boats

Materials

boats made from any of the following—milk cartons, match boxes,
plastic take-out food containers or styrofoam blocks

boat decorating and building items including—paper, stick on reinforcements for paper, clear contact paper, plastic bags, foil,
drinking straws, craft sticks, cotton balls for smoke, toothpicks
or kebab skewers

white glue, masking tape, rubber bands or staples

water to float boats

string to pull boats

Art Process

1. Begin with a main form to use as the base of the boat such as a
   milk carton.
2. Attach parts to the boat using tape, glue, staples or other
   creative ideas. Decorate the boat too.
3. Go to a source of water such as a puddle, pond, children's
   plastic swim pool or quiet creek.
4. Attach a string to the boat and launch the boat. Pull the boat as
   desired.

Variations

- Name the boats.
- Have a boat show or "Boats Afloat Celebration."
- Push the boat along with a stick instead of a string.

YARN PULL ATTACHED →
WITH TAPE AND
STAPLES

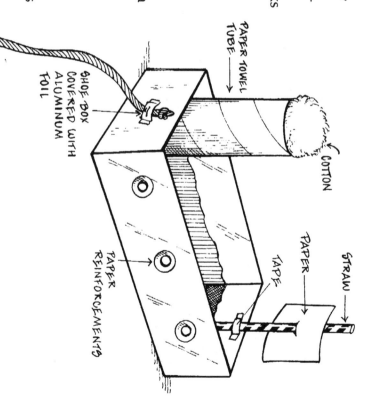

PAPER TOWEL
TUBE

COTTON

SHOE BOX
COVERED WITH
ALUMINUM
FOIL

PAPER
REINFORCEMENTS

STRAW

PAPER

TAPE

HINT

- Some boats will not float too well so young artists
  may wish to test their boats in the sink, make adjust-
  ments and launch their boat after sufficient
  testing.
- Masking tape holds very well even when wet;
  cellophane tape does not.

Stick Wrapping

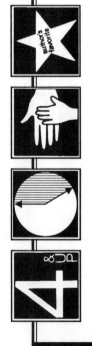

Materials

3' (1 m) stick or 1/2"-3/4" (1.5 -2 cm) dowel

many colors and lengths of yarn, string, ribbon or streamers,
embroidery floss, fabric strips and other string-like materials

decorations such as feathers, felt, foil or flowers with stems

glue

masking tape

Art Process

1. Start wrapping the stick with yarn. With adult help, tie a half-hitch knot at the beginning or use masking tape to attach the yarn securely to the stick.

2. Continue wrapping the chosen material tightly around the stick.

3. Change colors at any time. The new yarn can either be tied to the previous piece of yarn or taped to the stick. Begin to wrap the stick with the new color, texture or material. Loose ends can be left hanging or neatly tucked in. Encourage creativity.

4. As wrapping continues, other decorative items can be tied, taped, glued or wrapped into the yarn or string. This gives the wrapping a "surprise" character that makes it unique.

5. Loose ends can also be decorated with any interesting items.

Variation

- Find a pole, pillar or column to wrap with larger strips of fabric, colored ropes and yarn for a large rendition of the wrapped stick.

FLOWER

BEADS

EMBROIDERY FLOSS

FELT LEAVES

WEEDS

FOIL UNDERNEATH

RIBBON

SMALL FLEXIBLE BRANCHES WITH LEAVES

YARN

HINT

- Wrapping tightly can be difficult for some artists. Use lots of tape or tying to help attach the yarn to the stick.

- Shorter sticks work well for younger children. Working in pairs can be helpful also; one artist wraps the stick while the second person holds the stick.

CONSTRUCTION

Paper Bag Kite

Materials

large paper grocery bag
string
stick-on paper reinforcements
hole punch
paints and brushes
white glue
paper scraps and collage materials
tissue paper
crepe paper
streamers
ribbons
paper liners for muffin tins or candy cups

Art Process

1. Punch four holes in the paper bag, one on each of the four corners about one-half inch from the edge of the bag.
2. Stick a reinforcement circle on each hole.
3. Cut two pieces of string to about 36" in (1 m) length. Tie each end of one string into a reinforced hole to form a loop. Make a loop with the second string.
4. Cut another piece of string to about 36" (1 m) long. Put it through the two loops and tie it. (This will be the kite handle.)
5. Paint the bag as desired. Allow the paint to completely dry.
6. Glue paper collage materials and streamers to the paper bag kite. Dry the kite completely.
7. Open the bag. Hold onto the string and run. The wind will catch in the bag and the kite will fly out and above the artist.

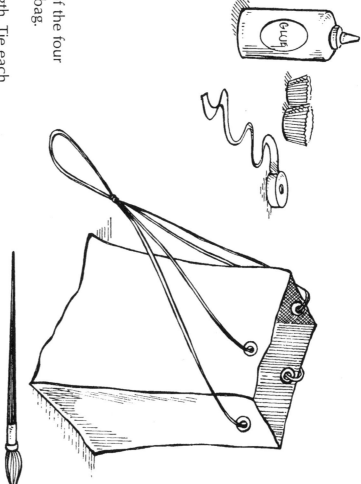

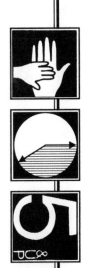

HINT

• For the strongest and most successful kite experience, the bag must dry completely between painting, decorating and flying.
• Adult assistance is needed when tying the string to the bag but the decorating and flying is completely child centered.
• Add extra reinforcements or clear contact paper to the holes to make the kite last longer.

CONSTRUCTION

Box Car

Materials

large cardboard box with top, flaps cut off
tempera paint, paintbrushes
paper plates
heavy string
foil
paper fasteners
stapler
tape
scissors
felt pens

Art Process

1. **Adult** cuts a hole in the bottom of the box large enough to fit over a child's hips.
2. Turn the box over so the hole is on top.
3. Paint the box using any designs. Allow the paint to dry.
4. **Adult** pokes four holes in the box with scissors for the car wheels.
5. To make wheels, push paper fasteners through paper plates and attach them to the holes in the box. Paint the wheels or decorate with felt pens if desired.
6. To make headlights, cover paper plates with aluminum foil. Attach the headlights to the box with tape or paper fasteners. Tape over pointed ends of fasteners inside the box.
7. **Adult** pokes a hole with scissors on either side of the top center of the box. Thread a heavy string or cord through one hole. Tie a double knot so it cannot slip through the hole.
8. After the young artist steps into the box car, pull it up to the waist. **Adult** pulls the string around the back of the child's neck and over to the second hole. Tie another double knot. Now the car "hangs" from the child's shoulders. The car is ready to drive.

HOLE IN TOP

BOTTOM OPEN

DOOR PAINTED ON

WHEELS

PAPER PLATES (WHEELS)

PAPER FASTENERS (BRADS)

HEADLIGHTS

HINT
- This project involves a lot of work, but the fun is worth the work. Let the children do as much for themselves as they can. Tying the string and poking holes in the cardboard is the most difficult part of the project and requires adult help.
- Be sure the box dries completely before using as a car. The paint will still tend to smudge off on damp or sweaty hands at play.

CONSTRUCTION

Project Index

Materials Index

Art Medium Index

The GIANT
Encyclopedia
of Theme Activities For
Children 2 to 5
Over 600 Favorite
Activities
Created by Teachers for
Teachers

A nationwide contest with thousands of entries produced this large book. There are 48 themes filled with more than 600 teacher-developed activities that work. From the alphabet and art to winter and zoo there are themes for every season and every day of the year.

All activities are clearly described and ready to use with a minimum of preparation. This is an ideal resource for a busy teacher. The book has a special strengthened binding which allows it to lie flat on a table. 512 pages.

ISBN 0-87659-166-7
19216

Gryphon House
Paperback

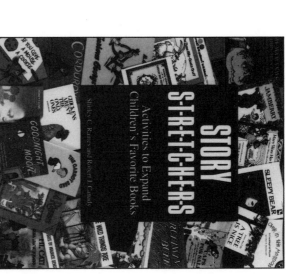

Story
S-t-r-e-t-c-h-e-r-s®:
Activities to Expand
Children's Favorite
Books (Pre-K and K)

*Shirley C. Raines and
Robert J. Canady*

It's original. It's fun. It's 450 terrific teaching ideas that are based upon the latest research on how young children become good readers. It connects 90 of the best children's books to every learning center-science, nature, math, art, music, movement, cooking, circle time.

Each book is "stretched" five ways with lively learning activities that heighten reading readiness and sharpen comprehension skills, too. And it's so easy to use! 256 pages.

ISBN 0-87659-119-5
10011

Gryphon House
Paperback

*Available at your favorite bookstore,
school supply store, or order from Gryphon House®*

Recommended Titles

Mudpies to Magnets
A Preschool Science Curriculum

Robert A. Williams, Robert E. Rockwell, and Elizabeth A. Sherwood, Illustrated by Laurel Sweetman

These 112 science experiments cover a wide range of topics, include the repetition that is needed for mastery and occur in a sequence that provides for growth and development. From "Pill Bug Palaces" to "Let's Get Soaked," the experiments here will delight and amaze children. 154 pages.

Gryphon House
Paperback

ISBN 0-87659-112-8
10005

More Mudpies to Magnets
Science for Young Children

Elizabeth A. Sherwood, Robert A. Williams, and Robert E. Rockwell

The hands-on activities will delight the imagination of young children. The science skills developed by projects in this book include classification, measurement, time and space relationships, communication, prediction, inference and numbers. 205 pages.

Gryphon House
Paperback

ISBN 0-87659-150-0
10015

Available at your favorite bookstore, school supply store, or order from Gryphon House®